THE
THANKSGIVING
TABLE

THE
THANKSGIVING
TABLE

RECIPES AND IDEAS
TO CREATE YOUR OWN HOLIDAY TRADITION

by DIANE MORGAN
Photographs by JOHN A. RIZZO

CHRONICLE BOOKS
SAN FRANCISCO

This Chronicle Books LLC paperback edition
published in 2006.

ISBN-10 0-8118-5542-2
ISBN-13 978-0-8118-5542-6

The Library of Congress has cataloged the previous
edition as follows:

Morgan, Diane, 1955-
    The Thanksgiving table : recipes and ideas to
    create your own holiday tradition / by Diane
    Morgan ; photography by John A. Rizzo.
    p. cm.
    Includes index.
    ISBN 0-8118-2991-X
    1. Thanksgiving cookery. I. Title.
TX739.2.T45 M67 2001
641.5'68—dc21
                            00-052331

Manufactured in China.

Designed by Efrat Rafaeli
Prop and food styling by Michelle Yurick
Styling assistance by Megan Savage

Distributed in Canada by Raincoast Books
9050 Shaughnessy Street
Vancouver, British Columbia V6P 6E5

2 4 6 8 10 9 7 5 3 1

Chronicle Books LLC
85 Second Street
San Francisco, California 94105

www.chroniclebooks.com

DEDICATION

To Greg, Eric, and Molly, for whom I give thanks every day.
And to Qerbie, my loyal companion in the kitchen.

ACKNOWLEDGMENTS

Writing a book about Thanksgiving has truly been a pleasure. Not everyone would find joy in cooking countless turkeys, or making mountains of stuffing and sweet potatoes, but I did. Thanksgiving is, by far, my favorite holiday of the year. Yes, all the foods associated with Thanksgiving are delightful and sumptuous, but it is the spirit of the holiday that moves me. Taking the time to give thanks, stopping to appreciate all the bounty in our lives, and sharing that with family and friends are what I most enjoy. Being able to express this in the form of a book has been a blessing, and there are many to whom I give thanks.

First, I am extremely grateful for the team of seasoned professionals at Chronicle Books. Bill LeBlond, cookbook editor, believed in this project from the beginning. I am deeply thankful for his skilled guidance, support, and dear friendship. Many thanks are given to Amy Treadwell, editorial assistant, for keeping this project on track. Deborah Kops, line editor for this book, was meticulously attentive to the details, and I am very grateful for that. Michele Fuller, publicist, deserves hugs and thanks for her responsiveness and enthusiasm.

I have been fortunate to work with John A. Rizzo, photographer par excellence, and his terrific team at Rizzo Studio. Many thanks to Donna Macdonald, Paul Rich, and John Valls; they kept me smiling and laughing through all the photo shoots. Michelle Yurick, food- and prop-stylist extraordinaire, has talents and imagination beyond compare. The beautiful dishes and linens used in the photographs were generously shared by Marci Taylor, Marti Kuhr, Priscilla Longfield, and Cheryl Acheson at Koko Kimono, and my friends at Carl Greve Jewelers—Lynne and Nick Greve, Geri Haber, and Sherry Ross. Thank you to the folks at Hunt and Gather, and A Place in Time for letting us borrow beautiful platters.

Recipe testing takes diligence, enthusiasm, and energy. I am deeply thankful to Marti and Morgan Kuhr for their skill and dedication. When developing recipes, I always need genuine feedback and advice. I am blessed to have the friendship of: Karen Brooks and George Eltman; Harriet, Peter, Eric, and David Watson; Mary Corpening Barber and Sara Corpening Whiteford; Holly and Brian York; Laurie and Peter Turney; Christopher and Susanna Brigden; Margie and Ken Sanders; Vance Selovar; Cam and Tony Kimball and their wonderful sons, Riley and Parker; and Cheryl Russell. Many thanks to all.

Finally, this book wouldn't have come to fruition without my husband, Greg. The love, unswerving support, and devotion you give to me are an incredible blessing—gifts beyond compare. Eric and Molly, my children, you have helped shape our family traditions, and enrich our lives every day. I am thankful for your love and deeply grateful for your support.

CONTENTS

INTRODUCTION

"OVER THE RIVER AND THROUGH THE WOOD
TO GRANDFATHER'S HOUSE WE GO.
THE HORSE KNOWS THE WAY TO CARRY THE SLEIGH
THROUGH WHITE AND DRIFTED SNOW . . .
HURRAH FOR THANKSGIVING DAY!"

Every Thanksgiving while I was growing up, my family did go over a river and over some hills to get to my grandparents' house for Thanksgiving dinner. It was a lively affair with twenty-three people around a big, long table, twelve being grandchildren. The youngest of us stared in awe at the big turkey, picked the crusty bread cubes off the top of the extra pan of stuffing, and giggled as we snatched pitted black olives from the relish tray and stuck them on our fingertips. My grandmother noticed every time, and knowingly asked, "So who ate all the olives?" We slyly put our hands behind our backs, shrugged our shoulders, and said, "We dunno know, Grandma," and then raced to the big staircase to nibble away. My childhood memories of Thanksgiving dinner are fond indeed—the flavors, the smells, the long buffet of food, and the big piece of pumpkin pie. It has always been my favorite holiday.

> > >

As a hungry-for-home-cooked-food college student, I rallied my friends in the dorm to make Thanksgiving dinner together. The small dorm kitchen had a motley collection of battered aluminum saucepans, chipped Pyrex baking pans, charred wooden spatulas, and slightly melted rubber ones. The dishes and silverware were mismatched, but nobody cared. We borrowed a roasting pan and some big mixing bowls from the college cafeteria. Several of us walked to the supermarket with empty backpacks and came back loaded down with a turkey, fixings for stuffing, sweet potatoes, broccoli, fresh cranberries, pumpkin pie filling, and ice cream. To the music of the Grateful Dead, we cooked and sang, laughed and danced, and ate a candlelit turkey dinner that lasted for hours. Red and gold maple leaves had been gathered and stuck into empty beer bottles for table decorations, and bandannas served as napkins. It was perfect.

Nineteen seventy-eight was the year I got married, and it was also the year of the twelve-pound turkey for two. What did I know—I was in my first kitchen, and this was our first Thanksgiving as a couple. We were far from family, missed the holiday traditions, and wanted to start our own. The smallest turkey we could buy was twelve pounds—seemed reasonable to us. So did six pounds of sweet potatoes and two bags of bread cubes for stuffing. No one ever told me that a turkey has two cavities (one is more obvious than the other), or that a packet of giblets could be found in the undiscovered neck cavity. After several calls home for advice and many hours of cooking, we dined sumptuously on enough food for about fourteen. As I recall, we fed on the remains of that same meal for many days thereafter.

As my children have grown into opinionated adolescents, they have helped shape the Morgan family Thanksgiving traditions. My daughter, Molly, insists that I bake the Spiced Pumpkin Pie with Pecan Pastry Crust (page 141); my son, Eric, requests the Italian Sausage, Mushroom, and Sage Stuffing (page 87) every time. My husband, Greg, still loves the Gratin of Fennel and Tomato (page 116), his all-time favorite side dish, after twenty years on our Thanksgiving table. Five years ago, I read about brining a turkey, made it that way, and have made it that way ever since.

This year has been different. This will be remembered as the year of endless Thanksgivings. In order to write this book I have cooked an unbelievable number of turkeys, made mountains of stuffing, and packed my freezer with bags of cranberries for fear of running out. I've had the pleasure of learning about the traditions of others, and sharing many of their recipes in this book. And I've been able to share my own traditions.

If this book spurs you to cook and host a Thanksgiving meal, whets your palate to try different recipes, entices you to decorate your table in new ways, then I will have done my job, and I will be thankful and grateful for that. Happy Thanksgiving!

A

HISTORICAL

PERSPECTIVE

ON

THANKSGIVING

We have many to give thanks to for the traditions of this holiday. The Pilgrims, arriving on the *Mayflower*, sighted land at the tip of Cape Cod on November 9, 1620. Sending a small exploring party in search of suitable habitation, the Pilgrims finally settled at Plymouth harbor on December 16, 1620. Their first winter in New England was devastating: They had lost 46 of the original 102 who had sailed on the *Mayflower*. But by the spring, a peace treaty was signed between the Wampanoag natives and the colonists, crops were planted, and the building of the settlement continued.

The fall harvest was a bountiful one, and the colonists decided to celebrate with a feast, inviting their Indian allies, Chief Massasoit and 90 Wampanoag natives, to dine with them. To the Pilgrims, this was a traditional English harvest feast, celebrating "the goodness of God" in providing for them; it was held so that they "might after a special manner rejoice together." This is the event that we have come to know as the first Thanksgiving, even though the Pilgrims had no name for it themselves.

Based on historical research by the Plimoth Plantation, the living-history museum of seventeenth-century Plymouth, the menu for this fall harvest feast consisted of:

Seethed (boiled) lobster

Roasted goose and boiled turkey

Fricassee of coney (rabbit)

Pudding of Indian cornmeal with dried whortleberries

Seethed cod

Roasted duck and stewed pumpkin

Roasted venison with mustard sauce

Savory pudding of hominy

Fruit and Holland cheese

The Indians brought five deer; Governor William Bradford sent "four men fowling" after wild ducks, geese, and turkey; and the foods of the harvest—corn, pumpkin, berries, and fruits—were made into stews and puddings. The Pilgrims and Indians, with their diverse cultures, came together as friends. They ate at large tables outdoors and competed in games testing skill and strength, keeping the celebration going for three days. What a party, what a potluck, and with games to boot—but no mention of football or who did the dishes!

Proclamations declaring a day of Thanksgiving were established in the seventeenth and eighteenth centuries, but not until 1777 did the Continental Congress declare a "first national Thanksgiving." All thirteen colonies joined in a celebration, though it was not yet a yearly event.

We need to give thanks to Sarah Josepha Hale, a magazine editor in the early 1800s, who wrote editorials in popular women's magazines promoting a national day for giving thanks "unto Him from whom all blessings flow." She doggedly wrote letters to governors and presidents until, finally, in 1863, President Lincoln proclaimed the last Thursday in November a national day "of thanksgiving and praise to our beneficent Father." The date changed only once, when President Franklin Roosevelt, deciding that Thanksgiving was too close to Christmas, moved the celebration to the third Thursday in November. The public responded with an uproar over this change (except for the merchants, who were thrilled about a longer Christmas shopping season), causing Congress to move Thanksgiving back to its original date two years later. Since 1941, Thanksgiving has been celebrated on the last Thursday of November.

From the first Thanksgiving onward, the true spirit and tradition of this holiday have carried on despite commercialism and the merchant-sponsored parades and football games. We celebrate together as family and friends in multi-generational, and often multi-cultural and multi-denominational gatherings, breaking bread together and sharing spirited times. Forty-five million turkeys unwittingly give their lives every year so that roast turkeys will grace our Thanksgiving tables. Cooks and "cleaner-uppers" spend countless hours in the kitchen for the benefit of their guests. For all of this, thanks are given.

FOODS

OF

THE

SEASON

Here is a list of seasonal foods and special ingredients for the recipes in this book, with tips on preparation and some preferences I would like to share.

BREAD CUBES

Not all bread cubes are created equal. My preference is to make my own for stuffing—it's simple and can be done ahead—using good artisan bread. I cut the bread into ½-inch cubes, which I prefer to the smaller size of store-bought cubes. (See page 88 for baking details.) Dry bread cubes purchased from an artisan bakery are my next choice, and commercially prepared bread cubes are an acceptable third. If you purchase the latter, look for unseasoned bread cubes and packages that haven't been crushed (or you will have lots of breadcrumbs instead).

BRUSSELS SPROUTS

Cute, like miniature cabbages, Brussels sprouts are typically sold loose, but some markets, especially farmers' markets, sell them on the stalk. Look for tightly packed heads with fresh green leaves, and avoid leaves that are yellowed or speckled with black spots.

CHESTNUTS

Fresh chestnuts are always in the market at Thanksgiving time. They are fun to roast and delicious to eat, but tedious to peel. There are about 36 chestnuts in a pound, yielding about 2½ cups of peeled nuts. For use in recipes such as a soup or stuffing, I often buy peeled chestnuts in vacuum-sealed packages, cans, or jars. (See the Cook's Note on page 32.) There are always trade-offs—buying prepared chestnuts is a time-saver, though not a money saver.

CHICKEN BROTH AND STOCK

I'm one of those cooks who always has homemade chicken stock in the freezer. It's a habit—every time I roast a whole chicken, I make a small pot of stock from the neck, giblets, and wing tips—and it never feels like a chore. Canned broth is a good substitute. Look for a brand that is low in salt; I prefer Swanson's low-sodium, fat-free broth.

CRANBERRIES

These are the small, red berries of a plant that grows in bogs on low, trailing vines. They are very tart in flavor and are always available fresh at Thanksgiving time. Cranberries come in 12-ounce packages; look for those with bright red, firm berries. Check the recipe carefully to see how much you need, and buy extra bags for the freezer. Cranberries are delicious in muffins, scones, and coffee cakes.

FENNEL

Also known as "sweet anise," fennel is a bulbous root, ranging in color from white to pale green, with stalks like celery and feathery tops. The root can be sliced and cooked or used raw in salads. The stalks, thinly sliced, can also be used in salads, and the feathery foliage makes an attractive garnish. The sweet anise flavor complements the traditional foods of Thanksgiving. This is a perfect do-ahead vegetable because it stays crisp-tender and reheats well.

NUTS

Used extensively during the holiday season, nuts keep best when stored in a tightly sealed container in the freezer. Toasting nuts brings out their delicate flavor and makes any dish to which they are added more delicious; it is worth the minimal extra effort. (See page 141 for toasting directions.) If you need ground nuts for a recipe, you can purchase them already ground or get shelled nuts and prepare them at home. Grind the nuts in a food processor fitted with the metal blade, using the pulse button to control the coarseness you want.

PEARL ONIONS

These tiny, papery white or yellow onions are used in side dishes, soups, and stews. They are more flavorful when fresh, but the frozen, already peeled ones will do in a pinch.

PERSIMMONS

Bright orange with a smooth skin, persimmons need time to ripen. They feel almost like mush when they are ripe and sweet enough to eat. Persimmons are in season in the late fall. You can buy them in quantity, and when they are ripe, scoop the soft, jelly-like flesh from the skin and purée and freeze it. Persimmon pudding is a fond holiday dessert for many.

PUMPKIN

For cooking purposes, skip by the big jack-o'-lantern pumpkins and look for sugar pumpkins, which have a sweeter and less fibrous flesh. To make your own purée, cut the pumpkin in half, scoop out the seeds, and roast it cut-side down in a 350°F oven until tender, about 45 minutes. When cool enough to handle, purée the flesh in a food processor. Canned 100 percent unsweetened pumpkin purée is a wonderful convenience if you're pressed for time.

SWEET POTATOES AND YAMS

Confusion reigns in the grocery store when it comes to sweet potatoes and yams. Technically, true yams are thick, starchy tubers native to Asia, Africa, and many parts of the Caribbean. They are unrelated to potatoes, including sweet potatoes, which are roots, not tubers. Yams are mostly found in Asian grocery stores—rarely in traditional American supermarkets. However, when you shop for sweet potatoes in a typical grocery store, you'll find yellow-fleshed sweet potatoes labeled "sweet potatoes" and dark-skinned ones with orange flesh labeled "yams." Those dark-skinned ones are technically sweet potatoes, too, and are mostly grown in North Carolina and Louisiana. The two varieties can be used interchangeably; however, the orange-fleshed sweet potatoes are higher in beta-carotene and sugar, so they are good for caramelizing. The yellow-fleshed sweet potatoes are higher in starch, so they are better for baking. For the recipes in this book calling for sweet potatoes, I prefer the dark-skinned, orange-fleshed ones.

WINTER SQUASH

These types of squash are allowed to mature on the vine and are stored for use in winter. The skin is hard and inedible, and the flesh needs to be cooked before eating. Hubbard, butternut, pumpkin, delicata, and acorn are some of the more common winter squashes in the market.

SPECIAL
EQUIPMENT
AND
TOOLS

I've cooked Thanksgiving dinner in an apartment kitchen with very little space and a bare minimum of equipment, and I've cooked the same meal in a dream kitchen with every pot, pan, and tool imaginable. Of course, I would certainly prefer to cook in a dream kitchen any day, but I learned from my Spartan experiences that some pieces of equipment are more essential than others when cooking a Thanksgiving meal, and it's not necessary to buy the very best. Review the list and see what you need before bringing home the holiday bird.

FOR THE TURKEY

ROASTING PAN

These are usually about 4 inches deep and made of stainless steel or aluminum, sometimes in a nonstick finish (makes for easy cleanup). The best ones are extra heavy and have sturdy, upright handles. Measure your oven before you buy! A medium pan, about 16 by 12 by 5 inches, is adequate for a turkey weighing up to 20 pounds. The best pans cost about $100 and will last a lifetime, but for years I managed with a black-and-white speckled, enamel-coated steel pan I bought at a hardware store for under $20. I don't recommend using the disposable foil pans, except for grilling, because they buckle so easily. If you must use them, buy two for double thickness; it will help.

ROASTING RACK

A V-shaped steel rack, preferably nonstick, elevates poultry and roasts for faster cooking and keeps the crisp skin intact. Buy one with a handle on each end; it makes lifting the turkey so much easier. The noncollapsible V-shaped racks are by far my favorite. A high-quality, medium rack costs about $20. Make certain the rack fits inside the roasting pan!

MEAT THERMOMETER

An instant-read meat thermometer has a small dial and a thin shaft, and registers from 60° to 220°F. Some are digital. These thermometers are not meant to be left in the oven—the dial is plastic and will melt—and should be washed after each time the bird is tested. A "must have" tool in the kitchen.

OVEN THERMOMETER

If you doubt the accuracy of your oven's thermostat, then buy an oven thermometer before you roast the big bird. Once you know how far off the thermostat is, you can adjust the temperature dial accordingly.

KITCHEN TWINE

Buy the proper twine to truss your bird. It is made of 100 percent linen, which resists charring. Flimsy string won't do, and dental floss (I've seen it used!) is a bad idea because it chars and can tear the skin. You'll be surprised how often you reach for twine once it's in the kitchen.

METAL SKEWERS

These are useful for closing the neck and chest cavity, especially if you are stuffing the bird.

BULB BASTER

This tool certainly makes basting a turkey easier, but a large spoon will work in a pinch. Buy either a stainless-steel baster or a heat-resistant plastic one. I prefer the latter because I can see through it. Glass basters are a mistake—they inevitably break.

GRAVY STRAINER

This looks like a measuring cup with a spout. It pours liquid from the bottom of the cup, and since fat rises to the top, the juice that is poured is relatively fat free. This is a handy tool for making gravy, but not essential.

CARVING KNIFE AND FORK

A carving set is lovely if you are presenting the turkey whole and carving it at the table. A set is not critical, but if you don't have one, it is important to have a very sharp utilitarian carving knife and carving fork. After working hard to roast the turkey, you will want to cut thin, even slices of meat. A good knife is a lifetime investment.

CARVING BOARD

Different from a cutting board, a carving board has a "moat" that collects meat juices and a "well" that traps them. This is handy for carving all types of meats and poultry. My favorite kind is a wooden board that is reversible, so you can use the flat side for chopping and dicing.

TURKEY PLATTER

All roasted up and nowhere to go? Make sure you have a platter large enough for serving your turkey.

FOR THE SIDE DISHES

LARGE MIXING BOWLS

I use an endless supply of mixing bowls while cooking for Thanksgiving dinner. My favorites are nesting stainless-steel bowls, though I keep a set of glass ones to use in the microwave. Stainless-steel bowls are inexpensive, easy to wash, and last a lifetime. Buy several in each size.

BAKING PANS

Count how many casserole dishes you'll need for your planned menu. Usually I need at least three 9-by-13-inch baking pans. The classic glass pans are great, though for looks I prefer the white porcelain ones. There are lots of attractive baking pans on the market, and they vary in price. Buy what fits your budget.

POTATO RICER OR MASHER, OR A FOOD MILL

If mashed potatoes are on your holiday menu, then you had better have a ricer, masher, or food mill handy. Food mills and ricers are the best tools for lump-free potatoes. The advantage of owning a food mill is that it is also great for fruit and vegetable purées; Foley makes a sturdy one. The old-fashioned mashers produce a coarser mash. (If you are contemplating using a food processor, don't—you'll produce potato glue.)

PEELERS, ZESTERS, GRATERS, JUICERS

All of these are handy tools and make cooking a lot more fun. If you don't own a rasp-like zester by Microplane, then buy one. This is my favorite new kitchen gadget. It outperforms other tools for zesting citrus, and works well for grating whole nutmeg and Parmesan cheese. I prefer two-piece juicers, either manual or electric, because the cup part catches the juice and makes it easier to measure.

FOR BAKING

PIE PLATES AND TART PANS

Check the recipe to make sure you have the right size before you start baking. Glass pie plates are inexpensive; I keep multiple 9- and 10-inch ones on hand. If you like to make tarts, pans with removable bottoms are also handy. Slip off the sides, slide the tart onto a pedestal cake stand, and you have a buffet-ready presentation.

PASTRY BLENDER, ROLLING PIN, PIE SERVER

For the pie and tart makers, good quality tools make baking a pleasure. Invest in a good rolling pin at least 12 inches long. It should be heavy, thick, and made of either hardwood or marble—it's a tool for a lifetime. While American-style rolling pins have handles at the ends, the French-style ones do not. Both work equally well; it's a matter of preference.

FOOD PROCESSOR AND STAND MIXER

These appliances are always handy in the kitchen, especially at holiday time. Save energy—make your pastry crusts in the food processor, and whip cream for garnishing in the mixer.

SOUPS AND SALADS

DELICATA
SQUASH SOUP
WITH PARMESAN
CROUTONS

SERVES 6

Delicata squash, as its name implies, is a finely flavored, richly sweet winter squash with a nearly fiberless flesh. Cylindrical in shape, with elongated ridges, this squash has yellow to pale orange skin with green striations. Its beautiful yellow flesh and delicate flavor make it perfect for this puréed soup.

Preheat the oven to 350°F. Brush the flesh of the squash with olive oil and place cut-side down on a rimmed baking sheet. Place the apples cut-side down on the baking sheet. Roast until tender when pierced with a fork, about 30 to 35 minutes.

Use a spoon to scrape out the flesh of the squash and apples, and put in the work bowl of a food processor fitted with the metal blade. Discard the skins. Purée until smooth. Add 1 cup of the stock and continue processing until smooth. Put this mixture in a $3\frac{1}{2}$- to 4-quart saucepan, add the remaining 3 cups of stock, and the cream, nutmeg, and sugar. Bring to a boil, and then reduce to a simmer and cook for 10 minutes. Add salt and pepper to taste.

TO MAKE THE CROUTONS

Place the bread cubes in a large mixing bowl. Drizzle with the olive oil, add the Parmesan, and toss the bread cubes until thoroughly coated. Spread in an even layer on a rimmed baking sheet and bake at 350°F until toasty brown, about 10 to 12 minutes. Set aside.

When ready to serve, ladle the soup into a warmed soup tureen or individual soup bowls, and garnish with the croutons.

2	pounds delicata squash, cut in half lengthwise and seeded
2	tablespoons olive oil
2	Granny Smith apples (about 1 pound total), cut in half lengthwise and cored
4	cups Chicken Stock (page 161) or canned low-sodium chicken broth
½	cup heavy (whipping) cream
¼	teaspoon freshly grated nutmeg
1	tablespoon sugar
	Salt and freshly ground pepper

PARMESAN CROUTONS

2	cups ½-inch cubes of French or rustic white bread, crusts removed
1	tablespoon olive oil
2	tablespoons grated Parmesan cheese

COOK'S NOTE

The soup can be made up to 3 days ahead. Cool and refrigerate, covered; rewarm just before serving. The croutons can be made 2 days in advance. Store in a covered container at room temperature.

PORTOBELLA MUSHROOM BISQUE

SERVES 8

Those oversized, dark, densely textured mushrooms you see sitting alongside the more delicate button mushrooms in the produce department are portobellas. They are delicious sliced and sautéed or grilled like a burger, and are perfect for a cold-weather soup. Portobella mushrooms are rich and meaty, which makes this soup aromatic and intensely flavored without the addition of a long list of ingredients. This is a perfect start to a Thanksgiving meal.

In a 6- to 8-quart saucepan, melt the butter over medium heat. Swirl to coat the bottom of the pan, and sauté the leeks and onion stirring constantly, until slightly softened and well coated with butter, about 2 minutes. Lower the heat, cover the pan, and cook for 30 minutes, stirring occasionally. Add the mushrooms, stir to combine, cover, and cook 10 minutes longer. Raise the heat to medium, stir in the flour, and cook 3 minutes. Add the thyme, bay leaf, stock, salt, sugar, and pepper. Simmer, partially covered, for 10 minutes.

Cool the soup slightly, discard the bay leaf, and then purée the soup in batches in a blender or food processor fitted with the metal blade. Return the puréed soup to the saucepan and add the cream. Cook over low heat until heated through, but do not let the soup boil. Taste and adjust the seasonings. Ladle the soup into a warmed soup tureen or individual bowls, garnish with the parsley, and serve immediately.

4	tablespoons unsalted butter
2	leeks, white and light green parts only, halved lengthwise and thinly sliced
1	large yellow onion (about 12 ounces), chopped
3	large portobella mushrooms (about 1 pound), wiped or brushed clean, and chopped
3	tablespoons all-purpose flour
1½	tablespoons fresh thyme leaves
1	bay leaf
6	cups Chicken Stock (page 161) or canned low sodium chicken broth
1	teaspoon salt
1	teaspoon sugar
½	teaspoon freshly ground pepper
1	cup heavy (whipping) cream
¼	cup minced fresh parsley

COOK'S NOTE

The soup can be made up to 3 days ahead. Cool and refrigerate, covered; then rewarm just before serving and garnish with the parsley.

ROASTED
CHESTNUT SOUP
WITH A MUSHROOM
GARNISH

Roasted chestnuts are a winter's treat. If you have never peeled
and eaten a freshly roasted chestnut, nor savored its aroma,
then make this soup. Although peeling 2 pounds of chestnuts
seems tedious, it can be done up to 2 weeks in advance.
The peeled, roasted chestnuts can be frozen, and then thawed
at room temperature for 1 hour before using.

Preheat the oven to 400°F. Using a sharp paring knife, make a long
slash on the flat side of each chestnut, cutting through the outer
shell and inner brown skin. Place chestnuts on a rimmed baking
sheet and roast until tender when pierced with a fork, about 1
hour. Every 15 minutes, sprinkle the chestnuts with a little water.

While the chestnuts are roasting, place the onions and carrots in
a 9-by-13-inch baking pan. Drizzle with the olive oil and toss the
vegetables so they are thoroughly coated. Roast until tender when
pierced with a fork, about 1 hour. Let cool while you peel the
chestnuts.

Peel the chestnuts while they are still quite warm, but cool enough
to handle. Using a sharp paring knife, remove the outer shell as
well as the inner brown skin. Discard any chestnuts that look rotten.
Set aside the chestnuts that are hard to peel and rewarm in a 400°F
oven; or place on a paper towel and rewarm in a microwave for
45 seconds on high. Repeat if necessary.

>>>

SERVES 12

2 pounds fresh chestnuts (about
   2½ cups peeled; see Cook's Notes)

2 large yellow onions (about 12 ounces
   each), cut into ½-inch thick wedges

3 large carrots, peeled and cut into
   1-inch chunks

3 tablespoons olive oil

8 cups Chicken Stock (page 161)
   or canned low-sodium chicken broth

1 teaspoon salt

   Freshly ground pepper

1 cup heavy (whipping) cream

Combine the chestnuts and roasted vegetables in a medium mixing bowl. Place one-fourth of the mixture in a blender or in a food processor fitted with the metal blade. Add 2 cups of the stock. Process until the purée is uniformly coarse rather than smooth in texture. Pour into a 4-quart saucepan. Repeat 3 more times with the remaining chestnut and vegetable mixture and the stock. Add the salt and a few grinds of pepper to taste. Heat to a simmer and cook about 20 minutes to meld the flavors. Add the cream, stir to combine, and remove from the heat. Taste and add more salt or pepper if desired. Keep the soup warm while you make the mushroom garnish, or cool and refrigerate, covered, up to 3 days prior to serving.

TO MAKE THE MUSHROOM GARNISH

Melt the butter in a 10-inch sauté pan over medium-high heat. Add the mushrooms, raise the heat to high, and sauté, stirring constantly, for 2 minutes. Add the thyme and parsley and sauté until the liquids evaporate and the mushrooms are lightly browned, 2 minutes longer. Set aside until ready to serve. This garnish can be made up to 2 hours in advance. Rewarm just before serving.

Ladle the soup into heated bowls, and mound a spoonful of mushrooms in the center of each bowl.

MUSHROOM GARNISH

2 tablespoons unsalted butter

8 ounces fresh mushrooms, such as shiitake, wiped or brushed clean, stems trimmed, and thinly sliced (see Cook's Notes)

1 teaspoon fresh thyme leaves

3 tablespoons minced fresh parsley

COOK'S NOTES

If you prefer not to roast your own chestnuts, you can buy peeled chestnuts in vacuum-sealed packages, cans, or jars at specialty-food stores. Drain any liquid in which they are packed. Prepared chestnuts are usually boiled rather than roasted, resulting in a bit of flavor loss. However, placing them on a rimmed baking sheet and roasting them for 15 minutes really improves their flavor.

If you can't find shiitake or other interesting mushrooms, use the brown mushrooms called "cremini" mushrooms found in most supermarkets. Use white button mushrooms as a last resort!

PUMPKIN, LEEK, AND
POTATO SOUP

Pumpkin isn't only for the dessert course. It is delicious in soup, and especially in this one, where the pumpkin is puréed along with potato and then flavored with hints of cinnamon and cayenne. Look for small sugar pumpkins rather than the large jack-o'-lantern variety. If you can't find any, butternut squash makes a good substitute.

Cut an 8-inch square of cheesecloth, and place the cloves, peppercorns, bay leaf, thyme, and parsley in the center. Bring up the ends to form a bag and tie securely with kitchen twine. Set aside.

In a 6- to 8-quart saucepan, heat the olive oil over medium heat. Swirl to coat the pan and sauté the garlic and leeks, stirring frequently, until softened but not browned, about 5 minutes. Add the cinnamon and sauté 1 minute longer. Add the chunks of potato and pumpkin, the stock, and the bag of spices. Bring to a boil. Reduce the heat and simmer, covered, until the potato and pumpkin are tender when pierced with a fork, about 20 minutes. Discard the bag of spices.

Cool the soup slightly; then purée in batches in a blender or food processor fitted with the metal blade. Return the puréed soup to the saucepan. Add the half-and-half, salt, sugar, cayenne, and freshly ground pepper to taste. Cook over low heat until heated through, but do not let the soup boil. Taste and adjust the seasonings. Ladle the soup into a warmed soup tureen or individual soup bowls, garnish with the minced parsley, and serve immediately.

4	whole cloves
10	black peppercorns
1	bay leaf
4	sprigs fresh thyme
4	sprigs fresh parsley
3	tablespoons olive oil
2	large cloves garlic, minced
3	leeks, white and light green parts only, halved lengthwise and thinly sliced
1	teaspoon ground cinnamon
1	large russet potato (about 12 ounces), peeled and cut into 1-inch chunks
1½	pounds sugar pumpkin or butternut squash, peeled, halved lengthwise, seeded, and cut into 1-inch chunks
4	cups Chicken Stock (page 161) or canned low-sodium chicken broth
2	cups half-and-half
1	teaspoon salt
1	teaspoon sugar
	Pinch of cayenne
	Freshly ground pepper
¼	cup minced fresh parsley

COOK'S NOTE

The soup can be made up to 3 days ahead. Cool and refrigerate, covered; then rewarm just before serving, and garnish with the minced parsley.

SPINACH, PEAR, AND
SHAVED PARMESAN SALAD

SERVES 8

A spinach salad, especially one with ripe fall pears, is a welcome addition to the Thanksgiving table. The salad can be served in a large bowl as part of a buffet, or on individual salad plates alongside the main course. With all the cooking you'll be doing, save yourself some time and buy the packaged, prewashed and trimmed baby spinach. The greens stay fresh for several days in the refrigerator.

Place the spinach and pears in a large serving bowl. Scatter the cheese on top.

TO MAKE THE DRESSING

In a small jar with a tight-fitting lid, combine the olive oil, vinegar, mustard, sugar, salt, and pepper to taste. Cover tightly and shake vigorously to blend the ingredients. Taste and adjust the seasonings.

When ready to serve, give the dressing a last-minute shake and pour over the salad. Toss gently to keep the pear slices intact, and serve immediately.

8	cups lightly packed baby spinach leaves, stemmed, rinsed, and dried
2	Bosc pears (do not peel), quartered lengthwise, cored and cut into long, thin slices
½	cup (2 ounces) coarsely grated Parmesan cheese (see Cook's Note)

DRESSING

½	cup extra-virgin olive oil
2	tablespoons balsamic vinegar
2	teaspoons whole-grain mustard
1	teaspoon sugar
1	teaspoon salt
	Freshly ground pepper

COOK'S NOTE

I prefer the taste of Parmigiano-Reggiano and recommend using it for this salad. To coarsely grate the cheese, use either the coarse side of a box grater or the medium shredding disk of a food processor.

BUTTER LETTUCE
SALAD with CHIVES,
TARRAGON, and
SATSUMA ORANGE SECTIONS

One of the jewels of winter fruit is the satsuma tangerine.
Satsumas are seedless, easy to peel, sweet, and succulent.
Paired with butter lettuce and a citrus vinaigrette, the tangerines
make a delightful addition to any Thanksgiving dinner.

Rinse the lettuce leaves and dry them in a salad spinner or pat
with paper towels. In a large mixing bowl (the bigger the better,
for tossing the salad), combine the lettuce and bell pepper.
Set aside until ready to serve.

Peel the tangerines and remove any white pith clinging to fruit.
Separate into sections, toss with the 1 tablespoon of the olive oil,
and set aside.

TO MAKE THE DRESSING
In a 2-cup glass measure, combine the olive oil, orange juice,
lemon juice, salt, sugar, and a few grinds of pepper to taste.
Stir well to combine. Add the chives and tarragon to the dressing.
Taste and add more salt and pepper if desired. Set aside until serving.

TO ASSEMBLE THE SALAD
Add the tangerine sections to the bowl of lettuce and peppers.
Stir the dressing to combine, pour over the salad, and toss well.
Divide among individual salad plates.

12	cups whole butter lettuce leaves (about 3 heads; see Cook's Note)
1	small red bell pepper (about 4 ounces), seeded, deribbed, and cut into matchstick strips
4	satsuma tangerines
1	tablespoon extra-virgin olive oil

DRESSING

½	cup extra-virgin olive oil
⅓	cup fresh orange juice (1 orange)
1	tablespoon fresh lemon juice
¾	teaspoon salt
2	teaspoons sugar
	Freshly ground pepper
2	tablespoons minced fresh chives
2	tablespoons minced fresh tarragon

COOK'S NOTE
I like to keep the butter lettuce leaves whole
for an attractive presentation. You certainly can
tear them into bite-sized pieces if you prefer.
If butter lettuce is unavailable, use a leaf lettuce
such as Green, Red Leaf, or a mixture of the two.
No matter what variety you choose, be sure the
lettuce is dried well; the dressing does not adhere
to wet lettuce.

ROASTED BEET
SALAD WITH WALNUTS
AND GOAT CHEESE

When the produce aisles and farmers' markets are brimming with root vegetables, I make beets—either golden or garnet red—the centerpiece for a perfect winter salad.

Preheat the oven to 350ºF. In a small bowl combine the walnuts, olive oil, salt, and pepper. Mix well to coat the walnuts. Spread on a rimmed baking sheet and bake until nicely toasted, about 7 to 10 minutes. Set aside.

TO PREPARE THE BEETS

While the walnuts are baking, wrap the beets individually in foil and place on another rimmed baking sheet. Bake at 350ºF until tender when pierced with a fork, about 1½ hours. Let cool for 20 minutes. Peel the beets by holding them under cold running water and rubbing off the skins. Cut into ½-inch wedges, and place in a large mixing bowl. Add the walnuts, onion, parsley, and basil.

TO MAKE THE DRESSING

In a 1-cup glass measure, combine the olive oil, vinegar, salt, sugar, and a few grinds of pepper to taste. Stir well to combine. Taste and adjust the seasonings. Pour over the salad and toss well. Marinate at room temperature for at least 1 hour. Just before serving, toss again and crumble the goat cheese over the top.

SERVES 6~8

½	cup walnut halves
2	teaspoons olive oil
⅛	teaspoon salt
½	teaspoon freshly ground pepper
6	medium beets, trimmed and washed
⅓	cup thinly sliced red onion
¼	cup coarsely chopped fresh parsley
8	basil leaves, cut crosswise into ribbons

DRESSING

¼	cup plus 2 tablespoons extra virgin olive oil
2	tablespoons red wine vinegar
¾	teaspoon salt
¼	teaspoon sugar
	Freshly ground pepper
3	ounces fresh goat cheese, crumbled

GOURD AND SMALL-PUMPKIN VASES

Make natural vases from gourds and small pumpkins for the holiday table, and fill them with autumn-hued flowers and leaves. These are pretty set on the burlap table runner, and you can use a scrap of the burlap to make a fringe collar.

Cut out the tops of the pumpkins with a sharp knife, and scoop out the pulp with a spoon. Line the pumpkins with foil. (Most pumpkins and gourds will remain watertight for several days, but lining them with foil gives added protection against leakage.) Cut the florist foam to fit inside each pumpkin, and add just enough water to saturate the foam. Arrange the flowers, grasses, and seedpods. Any tender flower stems can be secured and strengthened, using a wired pick.

TO MAKE A FRINGE FROM BURLAP
Measure the circumference of the pumpkin, and cut a strip of burlap 1 inch longer and 2 inches wide. Pull threads lengthwise, one at a time, to create 1 inch of fringe. Wrap the burlap around the top of the pumpkin vase and secure inconspicuously with a straight pin. Repeat for the other vases.

GOURD OR SMALL PUMPKIN GRAVY BOAT
If you are without a gravy boat for serving the giblet gravy, don't go scrambling to buy one. Make one from a small gourd or pumpkin. Cut out the top with a sharp paring knife, and then scoop out the pulp with a spoon. Set the pumpkin on a small plate or in a shallow bowl to keep it from tipping. Fill with gravy when ready to serve.

2 small pumpkins or gourds

Sharp paring knife or razor knife

Spoon

Aluminum foil

Florist foam

Scissors

Fresh and dried flowers, grasses, and seedpods

3-inch green, wired picks (available at florist shops or craft stores)

2 burlap strips (approximately 15 by 2 inches; optional)

Straight pins

CRANBERRY MOLDED
SALAD WITH
PINEAPPLE, CELERY,
AND ORANGE

For some families, Thanksgiving dinner wouldn't be the same without a cranberry-orange Jell-O salad. This is an updated version of my grandmother's recipe. She used a packaged Jell-O; I like to use unflavored gelatin and cranberry cocktail juice. This way I can control how sweet the mold is; I prefer it pleasantly tart, but not sharp or bitter—a perfect complement to the turkey.

I suggest using a decorative ring mold (mine is turban shaped), but there is no need to buy something special. A simple ring mold will work, and so will a small Bundt pan. If you don't own any of these pans, then use an 8-cup mixing bowl. This molded salad is such a beautiful garnet color, the shape of the pan doesn't really matter; just garnish around the base with some fresh cranberries or orange slices. It will look and taste great.

Pour 1 cup of the cranberry juice into a medium bowl. Sprinkle the gelatin over it, and let stand until the gelatin softens, about 10 minutes.

Meanwhile, in a 1-quart saucepan, bring the remaining $2\frac{1}{2}$ cups cranberry juice to a boil. Add the lemon juice and sugar and stir until the sugar dissolves. Slowly pour this mixture over the softened gelatin and stir until completely dissolved. Chill until partially set, about $1\frac{1}{2}$ hours.

In a food processor fitted with the metal blade, process the cranberries until coarsely ground. Set aside in a medium bowl. Add the oranges to the work bowl and process until coarsely ground. Add to the cranberries along with the pineapple and celery. Stir to combine. Gently stir into the chilled cranberry mixture. Spoon into an 8- to 9-cup decorative ring mold. Cover and refrigerate until cold and firm, at least 8 hours and up to 2 days.

To unmold, dip the mold into a large bowl of hot water for about 5 seconds. Dry the outside of the mold, place a serving platter on top, and invert the mold onto the platter. Serve immediately.

$3\frac{1}{2}$ cups cranberry juice cocktail

4 envelopes (¼ ounce each) unflavored gelatin

1 tablespoon fresh lemon juice

1 cup sugar

1 cup fresh cranberries

1 medium navel orange, including rind, cut into eighths

1 can (8 ounces) crushed pineapple, drained

1 cup finely diced celery

CELERY ROOT
SALAD WITH
MUSTARD VINAIGRETTE

I like serving this salad on Thanksgiving because it acts as a counterpoint to the rich and filling traditional foods. Celery root, also called "celeriac," is a type of celery grown for its root. This somewhat homely, brown and knobby vegetable tastes like celery, but its texture is more like raw carrot. Look for knobs that are hard and firm with no soft spots. Celery root can be served raw in salads, but it is equally delicious cooked and paired with potatoes in purées and soups.

TO MAKE THE DRESSING

In a small jar with a tight-fitting lid, combine the olive oil, lemon juice, mustard, salt, sugar, and a few grinds of pepper to taste. Cover tightly and shake vigorously to blend. Taste and adjust the seasonings.

In a large mixing bowl, combine the apples, celery root, and onion. Pour the dressing over all and toss to mix well. Add the parsley and toss again. Taste and add more pepper if desired. Cover and refrigerate. Bring to room temperature 1 hour before serving. Toss again just before serving. (This salad is at its best if made at least 8 hours and up to 1 day in advance, so that the flavors meld.)

DRESSING

½	cup extra-virgin olive oil
3	tablespoons fresh lemon juice
2	tablespoons Dijon mustard
1	teaspoon salt
½	teaspoon sugar
	Freshly ground pepper
3	crisp Granny Smith apples (about 1½ pounds), peeled, cored, and cut into ¼-by-¼-by-2-inch matchsticks
1	large celery root (about 2 pounds), peeled with a sharp paring knife and cut into ¼-by-¼-by-2-inch matchsticks
1	small red onion, cut into very thin wedges
⅔	cup minced fresh parsley

THE TURKEY

BUYING A TURKEY
THE CHOICES

At one time, fresh or frozen was the only choice you had to make when it came to buying a commercially raised, whole turkey. Now there are lots of choices, and quality and taste differences exist among the turkeys. Here are my thoughts on what's available in the marketplace.

STANDARD TURKEYS

These mass-produced, conventionally raised turkeys are sold either fresh or frozen during the holiday season. This type of turkey is a perfectly acceptable bird, easy to obtain without a lot of forethought from any large supermarket, and reasonably priced.

SELF-BASTING TURKEYS

These turkeys, sold fresh or frozen, have been "enhanced" with fat of some sort, in addition to natural and artificial flavorings. The theory behind this product is to make a turkey that doesn't need to be basted, saving the cook time and energy. Good idea in theory, badly executed in practice, primarily because the enhancer is flavored vegetable oil, which is not an enhancer in my opinion. Honestly, this is my least favorite turkey on the market. Do not brine a self-basting turkey. These birds have been injected with a salt solution.

FREE-RANGE TURKEYS

These are the turkeys that get to run around the barnyard, so to speak. They aren't necessarily raised outdoors, but they are raised in spacious, open environments. These are unquestionably more expensive turkeys, but they can be delicious, moist, and flavorful birds, and, in my opinion, may be worth the price. Free-range turkeys are often organic (and, therefore, costlier still).

KOSHER TURKEYS

They are usually sold frozen, but in large supermarkets, they are often available fresh at Thanksgiving. These turkeys have been inspected, slaughtered, and cleaned under strict rabbinical supervision, which makes for an expensive bird. For observant Jewish guests, these are the birds to buy; otherwise, I'd opt for a nonkosher, free-range one. Do not brine a kosher turkey. These birds have already been salted in the koshering process.

"WILD" TURKEYS

The only way you are going to get a true wild turkey is to shoot one yourself or cultivate a friend who hunts. Most turkeys labeled "wild" by specialty producers are farm raised. These turkeys are expensive, the meat tends to be tough, and the flavor doesn't justify the price. Smile if a friend calls with one freshly killed and cleaned; roast the breast meat and stew the dark meat.

FRESH OR FROZEN?

Whether it's fresh or frozen, it takes planning when it comes to buying a turkey. Buying a fresh turkey, especially a free-range one, requires a call to the butcher shop or grocery store at least one or two weeks ahead. Obviously, stores like to know how much to order from the turkey producers, though I'm sure they pad their orders for those last-minute, oy-I-forgot-to-order-a-turkey shoppers. However, you can't assume there will be a turkey waiting for you, so mark your calendar.

The convenience of not having to thaw a turkey for four to five days in the refrigerator is very appealing. Turkeys take up a lot of refrigerator space—usually an entire shelf—and that can be a burden on the cook and the refrigerator. The less time you spend juggling shelf space and monitoring the defrosting turkey, the better. In addition, fresh turkeys are more moist because the meat hasn't dried out from being frozen. And that's the bottom line—a fresh turkey is a better product overall.

If, for whatever reason—price, convenience, timing, a supermarket freebie—you buy a frozen turkey, you still need to plan ahead. The turkey may be at home with you, but it needs to be thawed carefully and slowly in the refrigerator for several days. See the chart below for defrosting times. If you're short of time, a turkey can be thawed in a sink or very large bowl filled with cold water, but that still takes a whole day.

DEFROSTING A TURKEY

To defrost a turkey in the refrigerator: Place the frozen turkey, still in its original wrappings, in a large pan with sides. Refrigerate until thawed according to the chart below.

To defrost a turkey in a water bath: Fill a sink or large bowl with cold water. With the turkey in its original wrappings, place the turkey in the water, covering it with as much water as possible. Thaw, changing the water occasionally, according to the chart below.

DEFROSTING TIMES

WEIGHT	IN THE REFRIGERATOR	IN WATER
10 TO 12 POUNDS	2 DAYS	4 TO 6 HOURS
12 TO 14 POUNDS	3 DAYS	6 TO 9 HOURS
14 TO 18 POUNDS	4 DAYS	9 TO 14 HOURS
18 POUNDS AND OVER	4 TO 5 DAYS	14 TO 24 HOURS

SIZE MATTERS

I knew if I gave this section a provocative title you'd read it! The size of the turkey you buy does matter, for several reasons. The most obvious, of course, is that you want to have enough for everyone. For turkeys weighing less than 12 pounds, figure on 1 pound of turkey per person. This allows for a reasonable amount of leftovers. Turkeys weighing more than 12 pounds have more meat per pound, so figure on ¾ to 1 pound per person, which leaves room for plenty of seconds and leftovers.

Size matters most when it comes to handling the bird. I have enough work to do on Thanksgiving Day without engaging in a wrestling match with a large turkey, so I avoid buying a turkey weighing over 16 pounds. (Even capable men will admit—

or maybe they won't—that maneuvering a hefty turkey is a lot of work.) If you have 25 people coming for dinner, my suggestion is to roast 2 smaller birds.

Another factor, which many people don't think about until it's too late, is that some ovens can't even accommodate a 25-pound bird. Measure and plan. Finally, a big turkey is impressive only if the bird and the cook make it to the dinner table in one piece. I nearly dropped a 22-pound turkey one year, inching it out of an oven barely large enough to accommodate it. So my advice comes from experience!

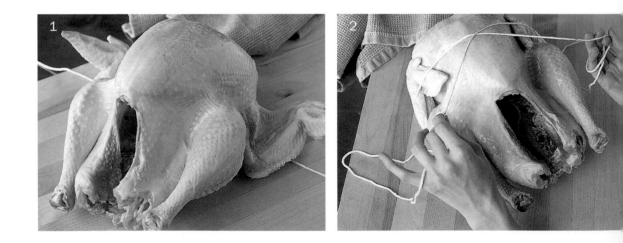

HANDLING A TURKEY
TRUSSING A TURKEY

Trussing a turkey means nothing more than securing the bird with string, skewers, or poultry pins in order to keep its limbs primly in place. This is basically a presentation issue. The turkey looks nicer with its wings tucked in close to the breast, and its legs demurely closed. And, honestly, it is easier to turn the turkey while roasting it when it is securely tied. I own a trussing needle but hardly use it. It is easy, and quite effective, to just tie the bird with some cotton kitchen twine using the following method. Though I prefer to roast an unstuffed turkey (because I like stuffing that is crispy and beautifully browned in its own dish), here are directions for trussing both a stuffed and unstuffed bird.

TO TRUSS AN UNSTUFFED TURKEY

Have ready one 4-foot length of kitchen twine. Place the turkey on a work surface with the legs facing you. Center the twine across the back (under the shoulders) of the turkey. Make sure the flap of neck skin covers the neck cavity and is secured by the twine. With an end in each hand, pull the string up over the top of the breast, tightening it so that the wings are drawn in close to the body; then cross over the two ends and tie. Now bring the twine down to the legs, bring the legs together, wrap the string around the ends (knobs) of the legs, and tie a knot. Trim any extra length of string.

TO TRUSS A STUFFED TURKEY

Have ready one 4-foot length of kitchen twine and one 1-foot length, plus thin metal skewers, or poultry pins. Loosely fill both the neck and chest cavities with stuffing.* (Stuffing expands when heated, which is why you don't want it tightly packed in the cavities. Put any extra stuffing in a buttered baking pan and bake it separately.) Pull the flap of neck skin over the stuffed neck cavity and secure it to the body with a skewer. Now pull the skin together on either side of the chest cavity, and close securely with 3 or 4 metal skewers. Using the shorter piece of twine, tie a knot around the tail. Lace the twine up the skewers, from bottom to top, as if lacing a shoe; then knot the ends of the string together. Cut off the excess string. Use the 4-foot length to tie the rest of the bird as directed in the instructions for trussing an unstuffed turkey.

* The stuffing should be at room temperature. Cold stuffing, when packed inside the turkey, may not reach 165°F (the temperature it needs to reach to avoid harmful bacteria from developing) by the time the turkey is done.

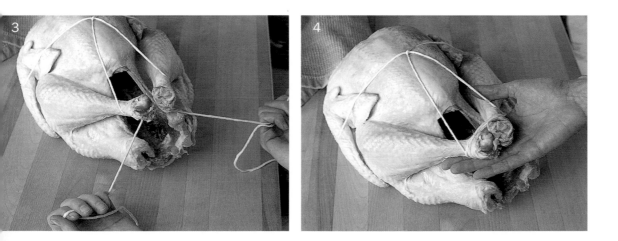

ROASTING TIMES

The times listed below are based on an oven temperature of 500°F for the first 30 minutes, and 350°F for the remainder of the roasting time. The turkey is roasted (using a V-shaped roasting rack) breast-side down for 1 hour, then turned and roasted breast-side up for the remainder of the cooking time. This method produces an evenly browned, beautiful turkey with crisp skin and moist meat.

The turkey is done when an instant-read meat thermometer inserted into the thickest part of the thigh registers 165° to 170°F. Allow the turkey to rest, with tented foil to keep it warm, for 15 to 30 minutes before carving.

WEIGHT	UNSTUFFED TURKEY	STUFFED TURKEY
10 TO 12 POUNDS	1¾ TO 2 HOURS	2 TO 2¼ HOURS
12 TO 14 POUNDS	2 TO 2½ HOURS	2¼ TO 3 HOURS
14 TO 18 POUNDS	2½ TO 3 HOURS	2¾ TO 3½ HOURS
18 POUNDS AND OVER	3½ HOURS+	4 HOURS+

CARVING A TURKEY

If you are a confident turkey carver, place the turkey on a large serving platter and carve it at the table. For the majority of us, carving the turkey in the kitchen is a safer bet. Place the turkey on a carving board, ideally one that has a moat and well to catch the delicious poultry juices. Untie the bird and remove all skewers. Using a sharp carving knife and meat fork, cut down between the thigh and body until you feel bone. Twist the leg and thigh a little until you see the thigh joint. Now cut through the joint to separate the thigh from the body. Cut the joint where the leg meets the thigh. Repeat on the other side. Now you have legs and thighs ready for a warm platter.

To carve the breast meat, start at the keel bone that runs along the top of the breast. Angle the knife and cut thin slices of breast meat from one side of the bird. Continue until you reach the rib cage; then carve the other breast. At this point you should have plenty of meat for serving. Lay slices of breast meat in an overlapping fashion down the center of the platter. Place the legs and thighs along the side. If a guest wants to have a wing, pull back the wing until you see the joint between the wing and the body, cut through that joint, and add the wing to the platter. Cover the rest of the turkey loosely with aluminum foil and remove the meat from the carcass later for some fine leftovers.

PRESENTATION

When considering presentation, the question you have to ask yourself is: do you want drama or ease of serving for Thanksgiving dinner? There is no right or wrong answer; it's a matter of what you are comfortable with. Presenting a whole roasted bird on a large, artfully garnished platter is a showstopper on a buffet or at the head of a dining table. Just remember, you'll need to study the section on carving so that you know what you are doing, and have an attractive carving set (a sharp carving knife and carving fork) ready for the task at hand. Play the part, and carve with authority and confidence. It's fun.

If you want to carve the turkey in the kitchen and present a platter of meat to guests, follow the carving directions on page 49, and garnish one corner of the platter or two corners diagonally opposite each other with some of the choices suggested below. Keep it simple; the presentation of fanned-out, overlapping turkey slices is beautiful in itself.

GARNISHES

I always like my garnishes to relate to the dish being garnished. For instance, when I make the Herb-Roasted Turkey (page 64), I buy or snip from the garden extra bunches of sage, thyme, and parsley. You can either tuck the herbs around the base of the bird or place them at the corners of the platter. For the Butter-Rubbed Turkey with an Apple Cider Glaze (page 66), fresh herbs look great as a garnish, and so do lady apples and kumquats nestled on top of the herbs.

See what's in your garden, if you have one. Interesting greens such as kale or savoy cabbage make beautiful garnishes. A quick trip to the yard and a few snips with scissors is all it takes. If you don't have a garden, peruse the produce aisles of your market for interesting seasonal produce. If the platter is large enough, small gourds and Indian corn nestled on herbs or greens look pretty around the edges of a serving platter. Just avoid the clichés—curly-leaf parsley with slices of orange, or parsley with pickled crabapples—and your turkey will look regal and festive.

BRINED TURKEY

Trust me here—you will never again complain, nor hear complaints, about dry breast meat if you take this easy first step in the preparation of your holiday bird. After nearly twenty years of cooking a Thanksgiving turkey, I am convinced that brining produces the most moist and flavorful turkey I have ever tasted. Brining requires nothing more than boiling water with salt, sugar, and spices; cooling the mixture; then soaking the turkey in the brine for 12 to 24 hours.

Have ready a heavy roasting pan large enough to hold the turkey. Place a plastic oven bag inside a second one to create a double thickness (see Cook's Note); then place these bags, open wide, in the roasting pan. Remove the turkey from its wrapping. Remove the neck and bag of giblets from the main and neck cavities of the bird. Store separately in the refrigerator for making gravy. If using the Apple Cider Brine, stuff the main cavity of the turkey with the orange quarters at this point.

Fold back the top third of the bags, making a collar (this helps to keep the top of the bag open). Place the turkey inside the double-thick bags, stand it upright, unfold the top of the bag, and pour the Juniper Brine or Apple Cider Brine over the bird. Add an additional 2 cups of cold water. Draw up the top of the inner bag, squeezing out as much air as possible; then secure it closed with a twist tie. Do the same for the outer bag. Place the turkey, breast-side down, in the roasting pan and refrigerate for 12 to 24 hours. Turn the turkey 3 or 4 times while it is brining.

Just prior to roasting, remove the turkey from the brine. Discard the bags, brine, and any cured herbs or spices remaining on the bird. Discard the oranges and ginger if using the Apple Cider Brine. Rinse the turkey under cold water and pat dry with paper towels. The turkey is now ready to be roasted.

MAKES 3½ QUARTS BRINE,
ENOUGH FOR A 10- TO 25-POUND TURKEY

JUNIPER BRINE OR APPLE CIDER
BRINE (RECIPES FOLLOW)

1   fresh or thawed turkey
    (10 to 25 pounds)

2   oranges, quartered (if you are using
    Apple Cider Brine)

SPECIAL EQUIPMENT

2   turkey-size plastic oven bags
    (see Cook's Note)

COOK'S NOTES

Plastic oven bags (made by Reynolds) are found with other food storage bags at supermarkets. Buy the turkey-size bags. They are food-safe; plus they are big, strong, tear-resistant, and come with twist ties. I do not recommend using plastic garbage bags because they are not intended for food storage. I use a double thickness of bags as a precautionary measure against leakage. For the same reason, I place the bagged turkey in a roasting pan.

The easiest way to crush whole spices is to use a mortar and pestle or a spice grinder. If you do not have either of these kitchen tools, then place the whole spices in a heavy lock-top plastic bag, seal the bag pressing out all the air, and pound them with the bottom of a small, heavy saucepan.

JUNIPER BRINE

Put all the ingredients in a 3- to 4-quart saucepan. Add 8 cups of water and stir to combine. Bring to a boil over medium-high heat, stirring until the salt and sugar have dissolved. Boil for 3 minutes; then remove from the heat. Add 4 cups of ice-cold water, stir, and set aside to cool. Then proceed with the directions for Brined Turkey (facing page).

APPLE CIDER BRINE

In a 3- to 4-quart saucepan, put the salt, sugar, ginger, bay leaves, cloves, peppercorns, and allspice. Add 8 cups of apple cider or juice and stir to combine. Bring to a boil over medium-high heat, stirring until the salt and sugar have dissolved. Boil for 3 minutes; then remove from the heat. Add 4 cups of ice-cold water, stir, and set aside to cool. Then proceed with the directions for Brined Turkey (facing page).

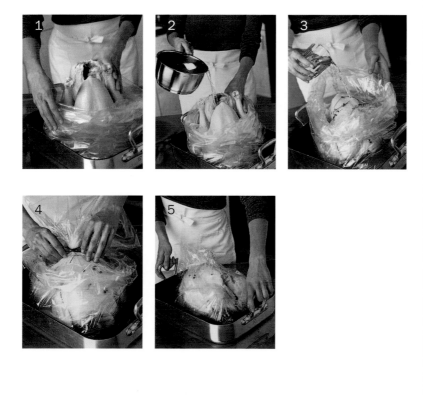

JUNIPER BRINE

⅔	cup kosher salt
⅔	cup sugar
5	fresh sage leaves
4	sprigs fresh thyme
2	bay leaves
6	whole cloves
1	teaspoon juniper berries, crushed (see Cook's Note)
½	teaspoon black peppercorns, crushed (see Cook's Note)
2	teaspoons whole allspice berries, crushed (see Cook's Note)

APPLE CIDER BRINE

⅔	cup kosher salt
⅔	cup sugar
6	quarter-size slices fresh ginger
2	bay leaves
6	whole cloves
1	teaspoon black peppercorns, crushed (see Cook's Note)
2	teaspoons whole allspice berries, crushed (see Cook's Note)
8	cups unsweetened apple cider or juice

BARBECUED
TURKEY

There are lots of great reasons to barbecue a turkey. If you are a one-oven household, barbecuing your Thanksgiving bird is the best way to free up oven space for all those pans of stuffing, sweet potatoes, and gratin that need to be baked. It is, guaranteed, a showstopping and delicious way to cook a turkey. There is no messy roasting pan or grease-splattered oven to clean up. It is a delightful cooking method for those living in a warm climate (but, hey, there are always those diehards who light up a grill whether it's raining or snowing). The hickory-smoked turkey leftovers are divine. *And,* barbecuing a turkey is easy. Make the giblet gravy if you like; it is delicious with the barbecued bird. Another option, simpler and still delicious, is to use your favorite bottled barbecue sauce and serve it warm alongside the bird. Be sure to allow 12 to 24 hours for brining the bird before you start cooking.

This grill recipe uses a technique called "indirect cooking" or "indirect grilling." This simply means that the food is not set directly over the coals or burners as it cooks in a covered grill. Essentially, this is grill roasting—heat rises and reflects off the lid and sides of the grill, circulating the heat. Indirect grilling is used for long, slow cooking; it is the best method for barbecuing whole chickens, roasts, ribs, and turkeys. The directions are for a gas grill with more than one burner, or a charcoal-burning, kettle-style grill with a vented lid.

One hour before you are ready to grill, place the hickory chips in a large bowl, cover with cold water, and soak. In the meantime, secure the legs of the turkey with a 1-foot length of kitchen twine by bringing the legs together, wrapping the string around the ends (knobs) of the legs, and then tying the string with a knot. Trim any extra length of string. Rub or lightly brush the turkey with olive oil. Place the bird, breast-side down, on the roasting rack, and set it inside the disposable roasting pan.

> > >

SERVES 12~20, DEPENDING ON THE SIZE OF THE TURKEY

1 Brined Turkey (12 to 16 pounds) made with Apple Cider Brine (pages 52–53)

Olive oil for brushing turkey
(about ½ cup)

SPECIAL EQUIPMENT

8 cups hickory chips

Kitchen twine

Sturdy, V-shaped roasting rack
(see page 22)

Heavy-gauge, disposable foil roasting pan
(large enough to hold the roasting rack)

Heavy-duty aluminum foil or a disposable aluminum pie plate

Drain the soaking hickory chips. Make 3 aluminum foil pouches or use the disposable foil pie plate. (Skip this step if your gas grill has a smoker box, and follow the manufacturer's instructions for using wood chips.) To make the pouches, cut three 16-inch-long pieces of heavy-duty foil. Fold each in half to make a pouch about 8 inches long, and fill with one-third of the wood chips. Crimp the edges together to seal, and then poke holes in the top of the pouch. If using a small disposable foil pie plate, fill it with one-third of the chips. (The pie plate will be refilled twice as the chips burn down.)

FOR A CHARCOAL GRILL

Forty-five minutes prior to grilling, prepare a hardwood charcoal or charcoal briquette fire. When the coals are covered with a gray ash, mound them on one side of the grill. Place 1 pouch or the pie plate of wood chips directly on the coals. Place the roasting pan on the cooking grate near, but not over, the coals. Close the grill lid.

FOR A GAS GRILL

Twenty minutes prior to grilling, preheat the grill with all burners on high. Turn off the burner directly below where the turkey will rest, and adjust the other burner(s) to medium-high. Place the drained wood chips in the smoker box, or place 1 pouch or the pie plate of wood chips directly on the heat source. Place the roasting pan on the cooking grate on the side of the gas grill that has been turned off. Close the grill lid.

Grill-roast the turkey for 1 hour. Open the grill lid. Add more wood chips if needed. With a wad of paper towels in each hand, turn the turkey, breast-side up, and arrange it so the leg and wing that were facing the fire are now facing away from it. Continue cooking, with the lid closed, for another 45 minutes. While the turkey is grill-roasting, begin the optional Giblet Gravy by making the stock (recipe follows).

Check the wood chips and add more, if needed. Turn the turkey once again so that the leg and wing that were facing the fire are now facing away from it. Continue cooking, with the lid closed, for another 45 minutes. Using an instant-read thermometer, check the internal temperature of the turkey by placing the thermometer into the thickest part of the thigh. Check both thighs. When the thermometer registers 165°F, the turkey is done.

Transfer the turkey to a carving board or serving platter, and cover the breast loosely with aluminum foil. Allow the turkey to rest for 15 to 30 minutes before carving to let the juices set. While the turkey rests, finish making the Giblet Gravy.

Carve the turkey, following the directions on page 49. Serve, accompanied by the sauceboat of gravy or barbecue sauce.

TO MAKE THE GIBLET GRAVY

Begin the gravy by first making a stock out of the giblets. In a medium saucepan, heat the oil over medium heat. Sauté the giblets until brown on all sides, about 5 minutes. Remove the liver and cool for 10 minutes; then cover and refrigerate. Add the onion, carrot, thyme, parsley, bay leaf, peppercorns, and 6 cups of cold water to the pan. Bring to a boil over medium-high heat, and then turn the heat to low. Skim any brown foam that rises to the top. Simmer the stock, until it reduces by half, about 1 hour. Pour the stock through a fine-mesh strainer set over a small bowl or 4-cup glass measure. Set aside the neck, gizzard, and heart until cool enough to handle. Discard the rest of the solids. Set the stock aside, and when the fat rises to the top, skim it. Shred the meat from the neck and add to the stock. Finely dice the gizzard, heart, and reserved liver, and add to the stock. Transfer to a small saucepan and set aside.

Bring the stock and chopped giblets to a simmer over medium heat. Place the flour in a 1-cup measure, add a small amount of simmering liquid, and blend until smooth. Slowly pour this into the gravy and whisk until thickened, about 3 minutes. Season to taste with salt and pepper. Transfer to a small bowl or sauceboat when ready to serve.

MAKES ABOUT 3 CUPS

GIBLET GRAVY (OPTIONAL)

2 tablespoons vegetable oil

Turkey giblets (neck, tail, gizzard, liver, and heart)

1 small yellow onion (do not peel), quartered

1 medium carrot (do not peel), cut into 2-inch chunks

2 sprigs fresh thyme

4 sprigs fresh parsley

1 bay leaf

6 black peppercorns

2 tablespoons all-purpose flour

Salt and freshly ground pepper

CLASSIC
ROAST TURKEY WITH
JUNIPER BRINE

SERVES 12~20,
DEPENDING ON THE SIZE OF THE TURKEY

This picture-perfect turkey will make a beautiful centerpiece for your Thanksgiving table. The skin will be crisp and golden hued, the meat will be moist (yes, even the breast meat!), and the flavor will be divine because you took care every step of the way. Brining is the answer to a moist turkey, and basting and turning it insures a fully browned and beautiful bird. Giving the bird time to rest after roasting (not you, just the bird) sets and seals in the juices. Your guests will be impressed!

Combine the onions, carrots, celery, garlic, sage, thyme, salt, and a few grinds of pepper in a medium mixing bowl. Mix well and set aside.

Position an oven rack on the second-lowest level in the oven. Preheat the oven to 500°F. Have ready a large roasting pan with a roasting rack, preferably V-shaped, set in the pan.

Put ½ cup of the vegetable mixture inside the neck cavity and 1½ cups inside the chest cavity. Scatter the remainder on the bottom of the roasting pan and add 2 cups of water to the pan. Truss the turkey following the directions for trussing an unstuffed turkey on page 47. Use a pastry brush to brush the turkey with half of the butter. Place the turkey, breast-side down, on the rack. Roast for 30 minutes. Lower the oven temperature to 350°F. Baste the turkey with the pan juices, and roast an additional 30 minutes. Remove the turkey from the oven. Using oven mitts covered with aluminum foil, or wads of paper towels, turn the turkey breast-side up. Baste with pan juices, and then return the turkey to the oven. Continue to roast, basting with pan juices after 45 minutes. After another 45 minutes, baste with the remaining butter. The turkey is done when an instant-read thermometer registers 165°F when inserted into the thickest part of the thigh. When the internal temperature of the turkey reaches 125°F, the turkey is about 1 hour away from being done. (Roasting times will vary, depending on the size of the bird, its temperature when it went into the oven, whether or not it is stuffed, and your particular oven and the accuracy of the thermostat. See the chart on page 48 for guidance.)

> > >

2	large yellow onions (about 12 ounces each), diced
2	large carrots, peeled and diced
3	large ribs celery, diced
4	cloves garlic, minced
7	fresh sage leaves, chopped
1	tablespoon fresh thyme leaves
1	teaspoon salt
	Freshly ground pepper
1	Brined Turkey (12 to 16 pounds) made with Juniper Brine (pages 52–53)
½	cup (1 stick) unsalted butter, melted

TO MAKE THE HERB-GIBLET GRAVY

While the turkey is roasting, begin the gravy by first making a stock. Put the giblets in a medium saucepan. Add the thyme, parsley, bay leaf, and peppercorns, and then add water to cover. Bring to a boil over medium-high heat, and then turn the heat to low. Skim any brown foam that rises to the top. Simmer the stock, partially covered, for 1 hour. Pour the stock through a fine-mesh strainer set over a bowl or 4-cup glass measure. Discard the solids. Set the stock aside, and when the fat rises to the top, skim it.

When the turkey is done, transfer it to a carving board or serving platter, and cover the breast loosely with aluminum foil. Allow the turkey to rest for 15 to 30 minutes before carving to let the juices set.

While the turkey rests, complete the gravy. Pour the reserved vegetables and pan drippings through a strainer set over a medium saucepan. Scoop out the vegetables from the cavities of the turkey and place in the strainer. Use the back of a spoon to press down on the softened vegetables, extracting as much liquid as possible, and pressing the solids through the strainer. Bring this mixture to a boil, skimming any fat that comes to the surface. Add enough reserved turkey stock to make about 2 cups of gravy. Boil until reduced slightly. If the gravy needs to be thickened, put the flour in a 1-cup measure, add a small amount of the simmering gravy, and blend until smooth. Slowly pour this mixture into the gravy in the saucepan and whisk until thickened, about 2 minutes. Season with salt and pepper to taste. Transfer to a small bowl or sauceboat to serve.

Carve the turkey, following the directions on page 49. Serve, accompanied by the gravy, and enjoy the results of your hard work!

HERB-GIBLET GRAVY

Turkey giblets (neck, tail, gizzard, and heart only)

2 sprigs fresh thyme

4 sprigs fresh parsley

1 bay leaf

6 black peppercorns

2 tablespoons all-purpose flour, if needed

Salt and freshly ground pepper

ROAST
TURKEY BREAST FOR
A SMALL GATHERING

Roasting a turkey breast is an easy and practical solution for a small Thanksgiving gathering. It's quick to roast, makes a lovely presentation, whether you carve it at the table or serve it sliced on a platter, and there will be a manageable amount of leftovers. This turkey breast will be moist, beautifully browned, and brightly flavored with lemon juice and fresh herbs.

Preheat the oven to 375°F. Trim any visible fat from the turkey breast, and save the neck, if included, for making gravy. Pat the turkey breast dry with paper towels. Place a rack in a roasting pan and set the turkey breast on the rack.

In a 2-cup glass measure, thoroughly combine the lemon juice, olive oil, rosemary, and thyme. At the top of the breast, slide your fingers back and forth under the skin to separate it from the breast meat, creating a pocket over the entire breast. Pour half the mixture inside this pocket, and the rest over the turkey breast, coating it well. Season the turkey with salt and pepper to taste. Set the turkey breast on the rack, skin-side up. Place the roasting pan in the lower third of the oven.

Roast the turkey breast, basting every 30 minutes, until the juices run clear when a sharp knife is inserted into the thickest part of the breast, or when an instant-read thermometer, inserted in the same spot and not touching bone, registers 165°F, about $1\frac{1}{4}$ to $1\frac{1}{2}$ hours. Remove the turkey breast from the oven, place on a carving board, cover the breast loosely with aluminum foil, and let rest for 10 minutes.

TO MAKE THE GRAVY

While the turkey is resting, make a quick gravy. In a small jar with a tight-fitting lid, mix together the flour and 2 tablespoons of the chicken stock. Place the roasting pan over medium heat, add the remaining stock to the pan, and bring to a simmer. Using a wooden spoon, scrape and loosen any brown bits sticking to the bottom and sides of the pan. Shake the flour mixture again and add to the stock in the pan. Stir until the gravy is smooth and thickened; then ladle into a gravy boat or small bowl.

Carve the turkey breast and serve, accompanied by the gravy.

SERVES 6

1	whole (double) bone-in turkey breast (4½ to 5 pounds)
¼	cup fresh lemon juice
½	cup olive oil
3	tablespoons minced fresh rosemary
1½	tablespoons fresh thyme
	Salt and freshly ground pepper

GRAVY

1	tablespoon all-purpose flour
1	cup Chicken Stock (page 161) or canned low-sodium chicken broth

HARVEST CENTERPIECE

Look for a tin vase, or buy two of complementary sizes
at a craft store or florist shop. They are inexpensive and look
terrific, whether your table is set with heirloom china or
mix-and-match dishes.

Line the tin vase with the plastic liner, and then use a knife to cut
the florist foam to fit inside. Add just enough water to saturate the
foam. Use scissors to cut off the wire from 4 of the wired picks.
Puncture the bottom of a pumpkin or gourd and insert the flat
end of a wire pick. Do the same with the 3 remaining pumpkins
or gourds. Space them artfully inside the vase, poking the wooden
picks into the foam to secure them. Attach a wire pick to each ear
of Indian corn, wrapping the wire inconspicuously around the top.
Arrange the ears in the vase, securing the picks in the foam.
Trim the stems of the flowers and arrange them in the vase with
any grasses and seedpods. To complete the arrangement and fill
in any gaps, attach wire picks to the grape clusters and secure
them in the foam.

Tin vase

Plastic vase liner

Knife

Florist foam

Scissors

6-inch green, wired picks
(available at florist shops or craft stores)

4 miniature pumpkins or small gourds

Small Indian corn

Assorted flowers, grasses, and seedpods

Clusters of small grapes

HERB-ROASTED
TURKEY
WITH
GIBLET GRAVY

One of my favorite ways to roast a chicken is to tuck fresh herbs and butter under the breast skin and stuff the cavity with onion, garlic, and more fresh herbs. This is a classic French technique so why not adapt it to our American turkey and have a beautiful, buttery, Thanksgiving bird? Stuffing the cavity with onion, garlic, and herbs infuses the turkey with savory flavors. And the stuffing, baked separately, is crispy on top and wonderfully browned.

Position an oven rack on the second-lowest level in the oven. Preheat the oven to 500°F. Have ready a large roasting pan with a roasting rack, preferably, V-shaped, set in the pan.

Place the onion, garlic, 4 of the sage leaves, the 4 sprigs of thyme, and the sprigs of parsley inside the chest cavity of the turkey. Mince the 8 remaining sage leaves and combine them with the 2 tablespoons of thyme leaves and ½ cup of the melted butter in a small bowl.

At the top of the turkey breast, slide your fingers back and forth under the skin to separate it from the breast meat, creating a pocket over the entire breast. Pour the herb-butter mixture inside this pocket. Truss the turkey, following the directions for trussing an unstuffed turkey on page 47. Use a pastry brush to brush the turkey with the remaining ¼ cup of butter. Season the turkey with salt and a few grinds of freshly ground pepper. Place the turkey, breast-side down, on the roasting rack. Add 1 cup of water to the pan. Roast for 30 minutes. Lower the oven temperature to 350°F. Baste the turkey with the pan juices, and roast an additional 30 minutes. Remove the turkey from the oven. Use oven mitts covered with aluminum foil, or wads of paper towels, and turn the turkey breast-side up. Baste with the pan juices, and then return the turkey to the oven.

SERVES 12~20, DEPENDING ON THE SIZE OF THE TURKEY

1   large yellow onion (about 10 ounces), quartered

4   cloves garlic

12   fresh sage leaves

4   sprigs fresh thyme plus 2 tablespoons fresh thyme leaves

4   sprigs fresh parsley

1   Brined Turkey (12 to 16 pounds) made with Juniper Brine (page 53)

¾   cup (1½ sticks) unsalted butter, melted

2   teaspoons kosher salt

Freshly ground pepper

Giblet Gravy (page 57)

Continue to roast the turkey, basting occasionally. The turkey is done when an instant-read thermometer registers 165°F when inserted into the thickest part of the thigh. When the internal temperature of the turkey reaches 125°F, the turkey is about 1 hour away from being done. (Roasting times will vary, depending on the size of the bird, its temperature when it went into the oven, whether or not it is stuffed, and your particular oven and the accuracy of the thermostat. See the chart on page 48 for guidance.) While the turkey is roasting, make the Giblet Gravy.

When the turkey is done, transfer it to a carving board or serving platter, and cover the breast loosely with aluminum foil. Allow the turkey to rest for 15 to 30 minutes before carving to let the juices set.

Carve the turkey, following the directions on page 49. Serve, accompanied by the gravy.

BUTTER-RUBBED
ROAST TURKEY WITH
AN APPLE CIDER GLAZE

This turkey, cured with Apple Cider Brine (page 53) and then basted with apple cider during the last hour of roasting, has a sweet and beautiful bronze-glazed finish—perfect for showcasing on a buffet table. I like to garnish the serving platter with lady apples and kumquats nestled in a bed of fresh herbs. Pair this turkey with the Bread Stuffing with Apples, Bacon, and Caramelized Onions (page 91), and your guests will be returning to the buffet for seconds.

Position an oven rack on the second-lowest level in the oven. Preheat the oven to 500°F. Have ready a large roasting pan with a roasting rack, preferably V-shaped, set in the pan.

Place the onion, garlic, apples, thyme, and sage inside the chest cavity of the turkey. Truss, following the directions for trussing an unstuffed turkey on page 47. Use a pastry brush to brush the turkey with the butter. Season the turkey with salt and a few grinds of pepper. Place the turkey, breast-side down, on the roasting rack. Add the giblets, stock, and 1 cup of the apple cider to the pan. Roast for 30 minutes. Lower the oven temperature to 350°F. Baste the turkey with the pan juices, and roast an additional 30 minutes. Remove the turkey from the oven. Use oven mitts covered with aluminum foil, or wads of paper towels, and turn the turkey breast-side up. Baste with the pan juices, and then return the turkey to the oven.

SERVES 12~20, DEPENDING ON THE SIZE OF THE TURKEY

1	large yellow onion (about 10 ounces), quartered
4	cloves garlic
2	Golden Delicious apples, cored and quartered
4	sprigs fresh thyme
4	fresh sage leaves
1	Brined Turkey (12 to 16 pounds) made with Apple Cider Brine (pages 52–53)
½	cup (1 stick) unsalted butter, melted
2	teaspoons kosher salt
	Freshly ground pepper
	Turkey giblets (neck, tail, gizzard, and heart only)
1	cup Chicken Stock (page 161) or canned low-sodium chicken broth
2	cups unsweetened apple cider or juice
2	tablespoons all-purpose flour

Continue to roast the turkey, basting occasionally. After it has roasted for 2 hours, begin basting every 30 minutes with the remaining 1 cup of apple cider. The turkey is done when an instant-read thermometer registers 165°F when inserted into the thickest part of the thigh. When the internal temperature of the turkey is 125°F, the turkey is about 1 hour away from being done. (Roasting times will vary depending on the size of the bird, its temperature when it went into the oven, whether or not it is stuffed, and your particular oven and the accuracy of the thermostat. See the chart on page 48 for guidance.)

When the turkey is done, transfer it to a carving board or serving platter, and cover the breast loosely with aluminum foil. Allow the turkey to rest for 15 to 30 minutes before carving to let the juices set.

TO MAKE THE GRAVY

While the turkey is resting make the gravy. Place the roasting pan over medium-high heat. Discard the giblets. Skim any fat from the surface, and bring the liquid in the pan to a simmer. Using a wooden spoon, scrape and loosen any brown bits sticking to the bottom and sides of the pan. Place the flour in a 1-cup measure, add a small amount of the simmering liquid, and blend until smooth. Slowly pour this into the simmering liquid and whisk until thickened, about 3 minutes. Season to taste with salt and pepper. Transfer to a small bowl or sauceboat to serve.

Carve the turkey, following the directions on page 49. Serve, accompanied by the gravy.

VEGETARIAN
ENTRÉES

CHAPTER 3

ACORN SQUASH

STUFFED WITH

WILD RICE, CRANBERRIES, WALNUTS, AND HICKORY-BAKED TOFU

This is an adaptation of a recipe given to me by Stephanie Rosenbaum, a San Francisco–based food writer. Stephanie is a vegetarian, and this is her favorite Thanksgiving entrée. The festive combination of wild rice with sautéed vegetables, fresh herbs, toasted walnuts, and dried cranberries tastes great and looks pretty on the plate. The addition of hickory-baked tofu adds a rich depth of flavor that complements the wild rice perfectly. I suspect you'll have your turkey-eating guests asking for samples.

Preheat the oven to 350°F. Cut each squash in half crosswise. Scoop out and discard the seeds and strings. If necessary, trim the top and bottom so that the squash will sit level, and place on a rimmed baking sheet, cut-side up. Sprinkle each half with a little salt, pepper, and nutmeg to taste. Using 2 tablespoons of the butter, dot each half with some butter. Cover the pan with foil and bake the squash just until moist and tender, about 45 minutes.

Meanwhile, combine the rice, vegetable broth, ¼ teaspoon salt, and 2 cups of water in a medium saucepan. Bring to a boil over medium-high heat. Reduce the heat to a simmer, partially cover, and cook, stirring occasionally, until the rice is tender, about 40 minutes.

In a 10-inch sauté pan, heat the olive oil over medium heat. Swirl to coat the pan and sauté the onion, garlic, celery, and carrot until slightly softened, about 3 minutes. Cover the pan, adjust the heat to medium-low, and cook the vegetables until crisp-tender, 5 minutes longer. Add the sage, thyme, and parsley and sauté 1 more minute. Remove from the heat.

In a large bowl, combine the cooked rice, sautéed vegetables, tofu, walnuts, and cranberries. Taste and add more salt and pepper, if desired. Mound the rice mixture into the squash halves, dividing it evenly. Cut the remaining 2 tablespoons of butter into small pieces. Dot each stuffed squash with butter. Cover with foil. Bake at 350°F until heated through, about 20 minutes.

SERVES 8

4	acorn or dumpling squash
¼	teaspoon salt, plus extra to taste
	Freshly ground pepper
	Freshly ground nutmeg
4	tablespoons unsalted butter
1½	cups wild rice
1¾	cups canned vegetable broth
3	tablespoons olive oil
1	large yellow onion (about 12 ounces), finely chopped
2	cloves garlic, minced
2	large ribs celery, finely chopped
1	large carrot, peeled and finely chopped
1	tablespoon minced fresh sage
1	tablespoon fresh thyme leaves
½	cup minced fresh parsley
1	package (6 ounces) hickory-baked tofu, cut into ¼-inch dice (see Cook's Note)
¾	cup chopped walnuts, toasted (see Cook's Note, page 141)
¾	cup sweetened dried cranberries

COOK'S NOTE

Look for hickory-baked tofu in the refrigerator case of natural food stores.

LASAGNA
with SUGAR PUMPKIN, RICOTTA,
AND FRIED SAGE LEAVES

Please don't pass by this recipe just because the ingredients list is long and there are lots of directions. Yes, I admit it, there are several steps involved in making this lasagna (see the Cook's Note for a terrific time-saving suggestion). But trust me— it is worth every bite. The combination of sautéed pumpkin sprinkled with crisp bits of fried sage leaves, layered and baked between sheets of pasta, and covered with a creamy, herb-infused béchamel sauce, makes a splendid Thanksgiving entrée for your vegetarian guests. Once the various components are prepared, assembly is easy and, best of all, the lasagna can be made a day in advance, refrigerated, and then baked fresh for serving.

Cut an 8-inch square of cheesecloth, and place the bay leaf, peppercorns, thyme and parsley sprigs in the center. Bring up the ends to form a bag and tie securely with kitchen twine. In a 2½-quart saucepan, combine the milk and bag of spices and heat until hot, but do not let the milk boil. Simmer for 2 minutes; then remove from the heat and allow to steep while preparing the remaining ingredients.

Fill an 8- to 10-quart stockpot two-thirds full of water, cover, and bring to a boil over high heat. Add the 1 tablespoon of salt; then add the lasagna noodles, stir, and cook until al dente (cooked through but still slightly chewy), about 10 minutes. Drain in a colander, rinse with cold water, drain again, and reserve until ready to assemble the lasagna.

In a heavy, 8-inch sauté pan, heat the oil until it registers 365°F on a deep-fat thermometer. It should be hot, but not smoking. Have ready a baking sheet lined with a double-thickness of paper towels. Working quickly, fry one-third of the sage leaves for about 5 seconds; then, using a slotted spoon, transfer to the paper towels. Fry two additional batches. Set the cooking oil aside. Generously sprinkle the sage leaves with kosher salt, and reserve.

> > >

SERVES 8~10

1	bay leaf
6	black peppercorns
2	sprigs fresh thyme
2	sprigs fresh parsley, plus ½ cup minced
3	cups milk
1	tablespoon, plus 1 teaspoon salt
1	box (1 pound; about 19 strips) dried lasagna noodles (see Cook's Note)
¾	cup corn oil
½	cup fresh sage leaves
	Kosher salt
2	pounds sugar pumpkin or butternut squash, peeled, halved lengthwise, seeded, and thinly sliced
¼	teaspoon cayenne
	Freshly ground pepper
1	pound part-skim ricotta cheese
3	tablespoons unsalted butter
1	large clove garlic, minced
1	small yellow onion (about 5 ounces), thinly sliced
3	tablespoons all-purpose flour
¼	teaspoon freshly grated nutmeg
	Vegetable-oil cooking spray
1	cup (4 ounces) grated Parmesan cheese, preferably Parmigiano-Reggiano

In a 12-inch sauté pan, heat 3 tablespoons of the reserved oil over medium-high heat. Without crowding the pan, add slices of pumpkin and sauté until just beginning to brown, about 2 minutes. Turn, and sauté on the other side; then remove and drain on a baking sheet lined with paper towels. Continue sautéing the pumpkin slices in batches, adding more oil to the pan as needed. Sprinkle the sautéed pumpkin with the cayenne and add pepper to taste. Set aside.

In a medium bowl, mix together the ricotta and ½ cup minced parsley. Set aside.

TO MAKE THE WHITE SAUCE

Melt the butter in a 3½- to 4-quart heavy saucepan over medium heat. Swirl to coat the pan; then sauté the garlic and onion, stirring constantly, until just beginning to brown, about 2 minutes. Add the flour to the pan, stirring constantly, until the flour is blended and cooked through, 1 minute longer. Remove the spice bag from the milk, and slowly whisk in the milk, about 1 cup at a time. Bring the sauce to a simmer, and cook, whisking constantly, until it has thickened, about 5 minutes. Add the 1 teaspoon of salt and the nutmeg. Stir to blend, and taste and adjust the seasonings. Set aside.

Preheat the oven to 350°F. Coat a 9-by-13-inch baking pan with the cooking spray. Lay 3 strips of lasagna noodles lengthwise across the bottom of the prepared dish. Add half of the white sauce, and spread evenly. Place 3 more strips of pasta in the pan. Layer half the pumpkin slices evenly over the noodles. Crumble the fried sage leaves, and sprinkle half evenly over the top. Place 3 more strips of noodles on top. Use a rubber spatula to spread all the ricotta evenly over the pasta, and then add 3 more strips of noodles. Layer the remaining pumpkin slices over the top and sprinkle with the remaining sage. Add 3 more strips of pasta, and then spread the remaining white sauce evenly on top. For the final layer, add 4 strips of noodles and sprinkle evenly with the Parmesan. (The lasagna can be can be made up to 1 day in advance. Refrigerate, covered, and bring to room temperature 1 hour before baking.) Bake until bubbly hot and nicely browned at the edges, about 1 hour. Let rest for 10 minutes before cutting the lasagna into squares and serving.

THANKSGIVING CORNUCOPIA

Decorating and filling a cornucopia for your Thanksgiving table is easy and artful.

Use a wire cutter to trim the stems of the faux berries so they are about 2 inches long. Weave the wire stems through the rattan, encircling the opening of the cornucopia with the berries. Use thin wire, if needed, to secure and attach any berry clusters. Set the cornucopia on the table and mound miniature gourds or assorted fall fruits so that they overflow from the opening.

Wire cutter

6 to 7 strands assorted faux berries

1 to 2 rattan cornucopias
(available at craft stores)

Thin wire (30 gauge)

Assorted miniature gourds,
or small fruits, nuts, and berries

SPAGHETTI SQUASH

WITH ZUCCHINI,
GARLIC, AND TOMATO SAUCE

Spaghetti squash is a watermelon-shaped winter squash with a creamy yellow shell. When cooked, the nutty flavored, golden yellow flesh separates into spaghetti-like strands. With the right seasonings and a robust sauce, this novelty squash makes an attractive and delicious vegetarian entrée.

Preheat the oven to 350°F. Pierce the skin of the squash in several places with a sharp knife or carving fork. Place the squash on a rimmed baking sheet and bake until tender when pierced with a fork, about 45 minutes. While the squash is baking make the sauce.

In a 10-inch sauté pan, heat the olive oil over medium heat. Swirl to coat the pan and sauté the onion and garlic, stirring frequently, until softened and just beginning to brown, about 4 minutes. Add the tomatoes, adjust the heat so the sauce simmers slowly, and cook for 20 minutes. Add the zucchini and simmer 5 minutes longer. Add the parsley and salt and pepper to taste. Keep warm over very low heat.

When the squash is tender, halve lengthwise. Use a fork to scrape the flesh from the skin, and place the squash strands in a serving bowl. Toss with the butter, and season with salt and pepper. When ready to serve, spoon the tomato sauce over the top and sprinkle with the Parmesan cheese. (The squash can be prepared up to 1 day in advance. Refrigerate, covered, and reheat in a 250°F oven or in a microwave until hot. The sauce, without the addition of zucchini and parsley, can be made 1 day in advance. Bring to a simmer; then add the zucchini, parsley, salt, and pepper as directed above.)

SERVES 4~6

1   spaghetti squash (about 3 pounds)

¼   cup olive oil

1   medium yellow onion (about 8 ounces), cut into ½-inch dice

2   cloves garlic, minced

1   can (28 ounces) diced tomatoes in juice, drained (see Cook's Note)

2   small zucchini (about 8 ounces total), trimmed and cut into ¼-inch dice

⅓   cup minced fresh parsley

Salt and freshly ground pepper

2   tablespoons unsalted butter

½   cup grated Parmesan cheese, preferably Parmigiano-Reggiano

COOK'S NOTE

By November, the fresh tomatoes in the market usually have little flavor and a mealy texture. However, I have been finding fresh hothouse-grown beefsteak tomatoes in the market that taste pretty good. Substitute 2½ pounds beefsteak tomatoes for the canned tomatoes, if desired. Peel, seed, and coarsely chop them before adding to the sauce.

BUTTERNUT SQUASH
PASTITSIO
WITH ONION, TOMATO,
AND FRESH OREGANO

SERVES 8~10

Pastitsio is a classic Greek casserole dish layered with pasta, ground lamb or beef, grated cheese, tomatoes, and a cinnamon-flavored white sauce. I've taken liberties with this classic and turned it into a vegetarian entrée by substituting tempeh for the ground meat. For those not familiar with it, tempeh is a fermented soybean cake with a nutty flavor. When crumbled and sautéed, it is a perfect textural substitute for ground meat in a casserole, and it absorbs the flavors of the sauce. Like lasagna, making pastitsio requires several steps, but the dish can be assembled a day ahead and then baked fresh for serving.

Preheat the oven to 350°F. Brush the flesh of the squash with olive oil and sprinkle generously with salt and pepper. Place the squash, cut-side down, on a rimmed baking sheet. Roast until tender when pierced with a fork, about 35 minutes. Set aside until cool enough to handle. Scoop the flesh from the squash, place in a medium bowl, and mash with a fork.

TO MAKE THE TOMATO SAUCE

While the squash is roasting, start the tomato sauce. If the tempeh is not already steamed, leave it whole and steam over boiling water, covered, for 20 minutes. Crumble the tempeh when it is cool enough to handle. In a 10-inch sauté pan, heat the olive oil over medium heat. Swirl to coat the pan, and sauté the tempeh, stirring constantly, until it begins to brown, about 3 minutes. Add the onion and garlic, and sauté until slightly softened, about 3 minutes. Add the diced tomatoes and wine and bring to a simmer. Cover the pan, adjust the heat to medium-low, and cook for 25 minutes, stirring occasionally. Add the sugar, oregano, parsley, 1 teaspoon of the salt, and a few grinds of pepper. Taste and adjust the seasonings. Remove from the heat.

> > >

1	small butternut squash (about 1½ pounds), halved lengthwise and seeded
	olive oil for brushing
	Salt and freshly ground pepper

TOMATO SAUCE

6	ounces soy tempeh (see Cook's Note)
¼	cup olive oil
1	large yellow onion (about 12 ounces), cut into ½-inch dice
2	cloves garlic, minced
2	cans (28 ounces each) diced tomatoes in juice, drained
½	cup red wine
1	teaspoon sugar
3	tablespoons chopped fresh oregano
½	cup minced fresh parsley
1	teaspoon salt
	freshly ground pepper
1	tablespoon salt
1	pound dried ziti, penne, or bucatini pasta

While the sauce is simmering, cook the pasta: Fill an 8- to 10-quart stockpot two-thirds full of water, cover, and bring to a boil over high heat. Add the 1 tablespoon of salt; then add the pasta, stir, and cook until al dente (cooked through, but still slightly chewy), about 10 minutes. Drain in a colander, rinse with cold water, drain again, and reserve until ready to assemble the casserole.

TO MAKE THE WHITE SAUCE

Melt the butter in a 2½-quart saucepan over medium-high heat. Whisk in the flour and turmeric, stirring constantly, until the flour is blended and cooked through, about 2 minutes. Slowly whisk in the warm milk, about 1 cup at a time. Bring to a simmer and cook, whisking constantly, until the sauce has thickened, about 4 to 5 minutes. Add the cinnamon, nutmeg, the 1 teaspoon of salt, and pepper to taste. Stir to blend, and taste and adjust the seasonings. Whisk in the eggs, and set aside.

TO ASSEMBLE THE PASTITSIO

Coat a deep 9-by-13-inch baking pan with the cooking spray. Pour half of the white sauce into the pan. Spread half the pasta over the top, gently pressing the pasta into the sauce to thoroughly coat it. Spread half the tomato sauce evenly over the top. Combine the mashed squash with the remaining white sauce, blending it well. Spoon this mixture evenly over the tomato sauce. Spread the remaining pasta on top, gently pressing it into the sauce. For the final layer, spread the remaining tomato sauce evenly over the top. (The pastitsio can be can be made up to 1 day in advance. Refrigerate, covered, and bring to room temperature 1 hour before baking.) Bake at 350°F until bubbly hot and nicely browned around the edges, about 45 minutes. Let rest for 10 minutes before cutting into squares.

WHITE SAUCE

½	cup (1 stick) unsalted butter
½	cup all-purpose flour
⅛	teaspoon ground turmeric
3½	cups milk, warmed
½	teaspoon ground cinnamon
⅛	teaspoon freshly grated nutmeg
1	teaspoon salt
	freshly ground pepper
2	large eggs, lightly beaten
	Vegetable-oil cooking spray

COOK'S NOTE

Look for tempeh in the refrigerator or freezer case of Asian or natural foods stores. Read the labels on the backs of the tempeh packages and see if any come already steamed and ready to eat. It will save you the step of steaming the tempeh.

STUFFINGS, BISCUITS, AND MUFFINS

CHAPTER 4

CHEDDAR AND JALAPEÑO
CORN BREAD STUFFING

This is my all-time favorite stuffing to accompany Barbecued Turkey (page 54). The rich, smoky flavor of the turkey is a perfect match for the gutsy Cheddar and Jalapeño Corn Bread. For an extra kick, if you and your guests are spicy-food fans, dice a couple of fresh jalapeños and sauté them along with the onions and garlic.

If time permits, make the corn bread and hard-cook the eggs the day before Thanksgiving. The stuffing is even better when the corn bread has had a chance to dry out a bit, and the assembly will then seem like a snap.

Preheat the oven to 350°F. Coat a deep, 9-by-13-inch baking pan with the cooking spray. In a very large mixing bowl, combine the corn bread, bread cubes, and chopped eggs. In a 12-inch sauté pan, melt 2 tablespoons of the butter over medium heat. Sauté the turkey giblets, turning them to brown on all sides, until cooked through, about 5 to 7 minutes. Remove to a cutting board to cool.

Add the remaining 2 tablespoons of butter to the pan. Sauté the onion, garlic, green pepper, and celery until soft and lightly browned, about 5 minutes. Add to the bread in the bowl. Finely dice the giblets and add to the stuffing mixture. Add the beaten eggs and stock to the bowl, and mix well. Place the stuffing in the prepared pan and bake, uncovered, until the top is lightly browned and crusty, about 1 hour.

If you have room in your oven, bake the stuffing while the turkey is roasting. Otherwise, bake it beforehand and reheat it once the turkey is out.

	Vegetable-oil cooking spray
8	cups crumbled Cheddar and Jalapeño Corn Bread (recipe follows)
5	cups unseasoned dry bread cubes (see Cook's Note, page 88)
3	hard-cooked eggs, chopped
4	tablespoons unsalted butter
	Turkey giblets (gizzard, heart, and liver)
1	large yellow onion (about 12 ounces), chopped
2	cloves garlic, minced
1	large green bell pepper, seeded, deribbed, and chopped
3	large ribs celery, chopped
4	large eggs, lightly beaten
1	cup Chicken Stock (page 161) or canned low-sodium chicken broth

CHEDDAR AND JALAPEÑO CORN BREAD

Preheat the oven to 375°F. Coat a 9-by-13-inch baking pan with the cooking spray.

In a large bowl, combine the cornmeal, salt, sugar, and baking soda. Add the cheese, corn, jalapeños, buttermilk, and eggs, stirring just to blend. Stir in the melted butter. Pour the batter into the prepared pan, and smooth the top with a rubber spatula.

Bake until the corn bread is golden brown and a toothpick inserted in the center comes out clean, about 45 minutes. Let cool in the pan for 15 minutes; then turn out onto a wire rack to cool completely.

MAKES ONE 9-BY-13-INCH
CORN BREAD; ENOUGH FOR 8 CUPS
CRUMBLED, PLUS EXTRA FOR SNACKING

CHEDDAR AND JALAPEÑO CORN BREAD

Vegetable-oil cooking spray

2 cups yellow cornmeal

1 teaspoon salt

1 tablespoon sugar

2 teaspoons baking soda

1½ cups (6 ounces) grated sharp Cheddar cheese

1 can (15 ounces) creamed corn

½ cup canned diced jalapeños, drained

1 cup buttermilk

4 large eggs, lightly beaten

¾ cup (1½ sticks) unsalted butter, melted

BURLAP TABLE RUNNER

This is a project that requires no sewing. Burlap is inexpensive and creates a rustic, autumn look for your table. Measure your table before buying the fabric: 3 yards is enough for a standard, 6-foot table plus a 1-foot overhang at either end. Add ⅓ yard of fabric for each additional foot of table.

Steam the fabric if there are any creases. Fold in thirds lengthwise. Measure the length of your table, and cut the fabric so it is 2 feet longer. Pull threads on each end to create 1 inch of fringe. Arrange the runner on the table, centering it and adjusting it so there is a 1-foot overhang at each end. Cut the cording in half. On one end, use your hand to loosely gather the fabric about 3 inches from the bottom. Wrap the cording around several times, tie a single knot, and then finish with a bow. Repeat on the other end.

Approximately 3 yards burlap (45 inches wide)

measuring tape

Scissors

2 yards black cording (⅜ inch in diameter)

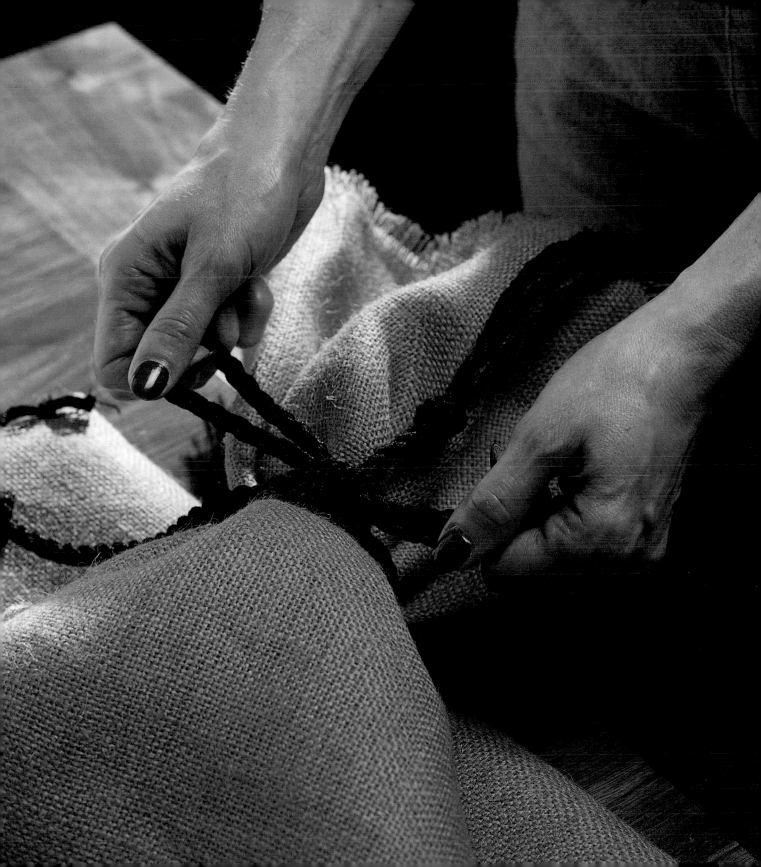

ITALIAN SAUSAGE, MUSHROOM, AND SAGE STUFFING

SERVES 12

Some are just "ho-hum, nothing-special" stuffings, but not this one. The sausage is key here. Where I live, several local butcher shops make their own savory and richly flavored link sausages, and those are what I buy. Look in your area for artisan sausage makers.

Once the sausages have cooked, I sauté the mushrooms in some of the flavorful fat. The browned bits of sausage clinging to the sides of the pan mix with the mushrooms, so that all these tasty morsels go into the stuffing. With the addition of sautéed vegetables and fresh herbs, this is bliss to a stuffing lover.

Preheat the oven to 350°F. Coat a deep, 9-by-13-inch baking pan with 1 tablespoon of the butter. Place the bread cubes in a very large mixing bowl. In a 10-inch sauté pan, heat the oil over medium-high heat, and swirl to coat the pan. Cook the sausages until nicely browned on all sides. Remove and let cool. Drain all but 3 tablespoons of the fat. Add the mushrooms to the pan and sauté, stirring frequently, until lightly browned, about 4 minutes. Add to the bread in the bowl.

> > >

5	tablespoons unsalted butter, softened
10	cups unseasoned dry bread cubes (see Cook's Note)
1	tablespoon olive oil
¾	pound mild Italian sausages
1	pound cremini mushrooms, wiped or brushed clean, stems trimmed, and quartered
1	large yellow onion (about 12 ounces), chopped
2	large carrots, peeled and chopped
2	large ribs celery, chopped
½	cup minced fresh parsley
1	tablespoon fresh thyme leaves
1	tablespoon minced fresh sage
1	teaspoon salt
	Freshly ground pepper
3	large eggs, lightly beaten
4	cups Chicken Stock (page 161) or canned low-sodium chicken broth

Return the pan to the heat, and add the remaining 4 tablespoons of butter. Swirl to coat the pan, and add the onion, carrots, and celery. Sauté, stirring frequently, until soft and lightly browned, about 5 minutes. Add the parsley, thyme, sage, salt, and a few grinds of pepper, and sauté 1 minute longer. Add this mixture to the bread cubes, and stir to combine.

Cut the reserved sausages into $1/4$-inch rounds and add to the stuffing. Add the beaten eggs and stock to the bowl, and mix well. Place the stuffing in the prepared pan and bake, uncovered, until the top is lightly browned and crusty, about 1 hour.

If you have room in your oven, bake the stuffing while the turkey is roasting. Otherwise, bake it beforehand and reheat it once the turkey is out.

COOK'S NOTE

Making your own bread cubes is a small, easy task with delicious results. There is just no comparison between homemade bread cubes and the cello-packaged ones available in supermarkets. I usually prepare mine a day or two before Thanksgiving. Buy a loaf of artisan or peasant-style bread, trim the crusts, cut the bread into ½-inch cubes, and spread them out on baking sheets. Toast the cubes in a 400°F oven until just beginning to brown, about 10 minutes. Cool completely and store in a covered container until ready to use. Artisan bakeries are springing up in every city and town around the country. Check out their breads, and use them for these bread stuffing recipes. However, if you are short on time, the bakeries often sell toasted bread cubes made from their day-old loaves, especially at Thanksgiving time.

WILD RICE
STUFFING WITH
PINE NUTS, DRIED APRICOTS,
AND FRESH HERBS

SERVES 8~10

Long considered the "caviar of grains," wild rice is native to North America, and it isn't really a rice at all. The grains are long, slender, and black with a unique nutty, almost smoky, flavor. They come from a reed-like aquatic plant that not long ago was found only in the wild but is now naturally cultivated. Local Indians still gather wild rice by paddling around in canoes in the rice beds of Minnesota. Wild rice also grows in the southern states of the United States as well as rural mountain valleys of Northern California. Wild rice pairs beautifully with game birds, chicken, and a holiday turkey. I like to serve this separately, but it is equally delicious stuffed in the bird.

In a medium saucepan, combine the rice, stock, and ¼ teaspoon of the salt, and add 2 cups of water. Bring to a boil over medium-high heat. Reduce the heat to a simmer, partially cover, and cook, stirring occasionally, until the rice is tender, about 40 minutes. (Not all of the liquid will be absorbed.)

Meanwhile, place a small, heavy skillet over medium-high heat. When it is hot, but not smoking, add the pine nuts. Stirring constantly, toast them until nicely browned, about 3 to 5 minutes. Transfer to a plate and set aside to cool.

> > >

2	cups wild rice
2	cups Chicken Stock (page 161) or canned low-sodium chicken broth
½	teaspoon salt
½	cup pine nuts
¾	cup dried apricots, quartered
5	tablespoons unsalted butter
2	large ribs celery, finely chopped
2	large carrots, peeled and finely chopped
1	medium yellow onion (about 8 ounces), finely chopped
1	tablespoon fresh thyme leaves
1	tablespoon minced fresh sage
½	cup minced fresh parsley
	Freshly ground pepper

Place the dried apricots in a small bowl, add hot water to cover, and allow to plump for 20 minutes. Drain and reserve.

In a 10-inch sauté pan, melt 4 tablespoons of the butter. Swirl to coat the pan and sauté the celery, carrots, and onion until soft and lightly browned, about 5 minutes. Add the thyme, sage, and parsley and sauté 1 more minute. Remove from the heat.

Preheat the oven to 350°F. When the rice is tender, add the sautéed vegetable mixture to the rice. Add the reserved pine nuts and apricots, and stir to combine. Add the remaining $1/4$ teaspoon of salt, and a few grinds of pepper. Taste and adjust the seasonings.

Use the remaining 1 tablespoon of butter to grease an oven-to-table casserole dish. Spoon in the rice stuffing and cover. Twenty minutes before serving, bake the stuffing until heated through. (The stuffing can be made up to 1 day in advance. Refrigerate, covered, and bring to room temperature 1 hour before baking. Increase the baking time to 40 minutes to insure it's heated through.)

BREAD STUFFING

WITH APPLES,
BACON, AND CARAMELIZED
ONIONS

Who can resist crisp bacon, sautéed apples, and the slightly blackened edges of caramelized onions? With the addition of savory herbs, this is the perfect combination for stuffing. Children, especially those (like mine!) who don't like mushrooms, really gobble this up. This stuffing pairs deliciously with the Butter-Rubbed Roast Turkey with Apple Cider Glaze (page 66).

Preheat the oven to 350°F. Coat a deep, 9-by-13-inch baking pan with the butter. Place the bread cubes in a very large mixing bowl. In a 10-inch sauté pan, cook the bacon over medium heat until crisp. Drain and add to the bread in the bowl. Remove all but 2 tablespoons of bacon fat from the pan, reserving the extra. Add the onions to the pan and sauté over medium-high heat, stirring frequently, until soft and lightly browned, about 5 minutes. Sprinkle the sugar over the onions and sauté, stirring constantly, until the onions turn golden and the edges caramelize, about 3 to 5 minutes. Add to the bread in the bowl.

Return the pan to medium heat, add 2 tablespoons of the reserved bacon fat, and swirl to coat the pan. Add the apples and celery and sauté, stirring frequently, until softened, about 5 to 7 minutes. Add the parsley, thyme, sage, salt, and a few grinds of pepper, and sauté 1 minute longer. Add this mixture to the bread cubes, and stir to combine. Add the beaten eggs and stock to the bowl, and mix well. Place the stuffing in the prepared pan and bake, uncovered, until the top is lightly browned and crusty, about 1 hour.

If you have room in your oven, bake the stuffing while the turkey is roasting. Otherwise, bake it beforehand and reheat it once the turkey is out.

1	tablespoon unsalted butter, softened
10	cups unseasoned dry bread cubes (see Cook's Note, page 88)
8	ounces bacon, cut into 1-inch pieces
1¼	pounds pearl onions, peeled and halved
1	tablespoon sugar
2	Granny Smith apples (about 6 ounces each), peeled, cored, and cut into ½-inch dice
3	large ribs celery, chopped
⅔	cup minced fresh parsley
1	tablespoon fresh thyme leaves
1	tablespoon minced fresh sage
1	teaspoon salt
	Freshly ground pepper
3	large eggs, lightly beaten
4	cups Chicken Stock (page 161) or canned low-sodium chicken broth

NAPKIN RINGS AND A DECORATED VASE FROM CORRUGATED CARDBOARD

Don't recycle corrugated cardboard—reuse it! Cut, and tied with raffia, it makes fun, texturally interesting napkin rings and adds a creative touch to a plain vase. Add autumn-hued fresh or dried flowers to complete the project.

TO MAKE A NAPKIN RING FOR EACH GUEST

Cut a strip of corrugated cardboard measuring 2 inches across the ridges and 10 inches down. This will create a natural roll. If available, use an empty paper towel roll as a form for making the rings. Roll the length of corrugated cardboard to form a ring, securing it inconspicuously in a couple of places with tape. Wrap 2 or 3 strands of raffia around the middle of the napkin ring several times, and then double knot it. Cut the ends so they are 1 inch long. If using dried flowers, cut the stems so they are 1½ inches long and slide them through the raffia to secure them. If using fresh flowers, wait until 1 hour before guests arrive to trim the stems and attach them to the napkin rings.

TO DECORATE THE VASE

Cut 1 piece of corrugated cardboard measuring 3 inches across the ridges and 15 inches down the ridges. This will create a natural roll. Roll the length of corrugated cardboard around the center of the vase. Secure it inconspicuously with tape. Wrap 2 or 3 strands of raffia several times around the middle and then double knot it. Cut the ends so they are 1 inch long or tie a bow and trim the ends. Slip 2 dried flowers, with the stems cut 1½ inches long, through the raffia to secure them. Arrange flowers in the vase.

Scissors

1 small roll corrugated cardboard or 3 sheets approximately 10 by 15 inches (available at craft stores)

1 empty cardboard roll from paper towels (optional)

Double-sided tape

18 to **26** strands Raffia

12 to **24** small dried or fresh flowers

1 glass cylinder vase (3 inches in diameter)

CHESTNUT, LEEK,
AND FRESH HERB
BREAD PUDDING

SERVES 12

For bread pudding lovers, this is a delicious alternative, or addition, to stuffing at the holiday table. Start with a crusty loaf of artisan bread: It can be white, sourdough white, part whole wheat, or a mixed-grain loaf. I trim the ends of the bread (and share those morsels with my food-obsessed dog), but I leave the rest of the crust on for flavor and visual interest. The rich, roasted chestnuts combined with the garlic and leeks makes this bread pudding robust and savory-sweet. For a buffet, bake the bread pudding in an attractive oven-to-table pan.

Dog-ear or mark this recipe page, and serve this bread pudding at Christmas or for other cold-weather festive occasions. It is perfect with roasted lamb or a prime rib roast.

Preheat the oven to 375°F. Coat a deep, 9-by-13-inch baking pan with 1 tablespoon of the butter. Set aside.

TO PREPARE THE CHESTNUTS

Use a sharp paring knife to make a long slash on the flat side of each chestnut, cutting through the outer shell and inner brown skin. Place the chestnuts on a rimmed baking sheet and roast until tender when pierced with a fork, about 1 hour. Every 15 minutes, sprinkle them with a little water. Peel them while the chestnuts are quite warm, but still cool enough to handle. Remove the outer shell as well as inner brown skin. Discard any chestnuts that look rotten. Set aside chestnuts that are hard to peel and rewarm in a 375°F oven, or place on a paper towel and rewarm in a microwave for 45 seconds on high. Repeat if necessary.

4	tablespoons unsalted butter, softened
2	pounds fresh chestnuts (about 2½ cups peeled; see Cook's Note, page 32)
1	loaf (1 pound) artisan bread
2	cloves garlic, minced
3	leeks, white and light green parts only, halved lengthwise, then cut crosswise into ¼-inch slices
2	large ribs celery, cut crosswise into ¼-inch slices
1	pound cremini mushrooms, wiped or brushed clean, stems trimmed, and quartered
½	cup minced fresh parsley
1	tablespoon fresh thyme leaves
2	tablespoons minced fresh sage
2½	cups Chicken Stock (page 161) or canned low-sodium chicken broth
4	large eggs, lightly beaten
2	cups heavy (whipping) cream

TO PREPARE THE BREAD

Trim off the ends of the loaf; then cut the bread into ³/₄-inch cubes. Spread them on 2 baking sheets. Toast in the oven until lightly browned, about 10 minutes. Set aside to cool.

TO ASSEMBLE THE BREAD PUDDING

Cut the prepared chestnuts in half. Combine them with bread cubes in a large mixing bowl. In a 12-inch sauté pan, melt the remaining 3 tablespoons of butter over medium-high heat. Swirl to coat the pan; then add the garlic, leeks, and celery. Sauté until soft and just beginning to brown, about 3 minutes. Add the mushrooms and sauté until lightly browned and just beginning to give up some liquid, about 5 minutes. Add the parsley, thyme, and sage, and cook 1 minute longer. Add the stock to the pan, and bring to a simmer. Add this mixture to the bread cubes in the bowl. Mix thoroughly.

In a medium bowl, whisk the eggs and cream together. Pour over the bread mixture, and stir to combine. Spoon the bread pudding into the prepared pan. Bake, uncovered, until the top is nicely browned and crusty, about 50 minutes.

If you have room in your oven, bake the bread pudding while the turkey is roasting. Otherwise, bake it beforehand and reheat it once the turkey is out.

SHIRLEY LeBLOND'S STUFFING

SERVES 10~12

Thanksgiving is all about hearty foods, taste memories from childhood, and regional traditions. My editor, Bill LeBlond, grew up in New England, where at Thanksgiving, a substantial meat-and-potatoes diet yielded a savory meat stuffing to accompany the holiday bird. James Beard favored a meat stuffing for the neck cavity of the turkey, and preferred to cook a bread stuffing in a separate pan. Bill's mother, Shirley, stuffs this recipe into the main cavity of the bird, but it could also be served as a separate side dish. Leftovers are terrific as a filling for baked stuffed peppers or acorn squash, or in a meat turnover with a caraway pastry dough.

Mix together the ground beef and pork. Crumble it into 4-quart stove-top casserole. Add water to barely cover the meat, and scatter the onion over the top. Cover and bring to a simmer over medium heat. Lower the heat and simmer for 1½ hours.

Twenty minutes before the meat mixture is cooked, boil the potato in a medium saucepan with salted water to cover. Cook until tender when pierced with a fork, about 12 to 15 minutes. Drain and return the potato to the pan; then mash well with a potato masher or put through a food mill.

Remove the meat mixture from the heat and use the back of a spoon to break up any large clumps. Stir in the mashed potato, the stuffing mix, salt, pepper, sage, thyme, and parsley. Taste and add additional salt and pepper, if desired.

1	pound lean ground beef
1	pound ground pork or good sausage meat
1	medium yellow onion (about 8 ounces), chopped
1	large russet potato (about 10 ounces), peeled and cut into quarters
1½	cups packaged herb-seasoned stuffing mix
1	teaspoon salt
1	teaspoon freshly ground pepper
1½	tablespoons minced fresh sage
2	teaspoons fresh thyme leaves
½	cup minced fresh parsley

OYSTER AND CRACKED-PEPPER CORN BREAD STUFFING

Not everyone grew up eating corn bread and oyster stuffing. I certainly didn't—but I love it now. Near Chesapeake Bay and in the coastal South, oysters go into everything from stews to savory pies to stuffing. The tradition dates from the nineteenth century, when oysters were cheap and plentiful; they were consumed with beer like peanuts are today. Now, they are neither cheap nor plentiful, but they are a delicious addition to corn bread stuffing. This is another stuffing that pairs beautifully with Barbecued Turkey (page 54).

Preheat the oven to 350°F. Coat a deep, 9-by-13-inch baking pan with the cooking spray. Cut the corn bread into ³/₄-inch cubes, and spread them out on baking sheets. Toast in the oven until lightly browned, about 10 minutes. Set aside to cool.

In a large mixing bowl, combine the corn bread cubes, dry bread cubes, and pecans. In a 10-inch sauté pan, melt the butter over medium-high heat. Swirl to coat the pan; then add the onion and celery. Sauté until soft and lightly browned, about 5 minutes. Add the thyme, sage, and cayenne, and cook 1 minute longer. Add to the bread in the bowl. Mix in the parsley, eggs, and stock.

Gently mix the oysters and their liquor into the corn bread mixture, being careful not to break up the oysters. Place the stuffing in the prepared pan and bake, uncovered, until the top is lightly browned and crusty, about 45 to 50 minutes.

If you have room in your oven, bake the stuffing while the turkey is roasting. Otherwise, bake it beforehand and reheat it once the turkey is out.

> > >

SERVES 12

Vegetable-oil cooking spray

1 recipe Cracked-Pepper Corn Bread (recipe follows)

2 cups unseasoned dry bread cubes (see Cook's Note, page 88)

1 cup pecans, toasted and coarsely chopped (see Cook's Note, page 141)

4 tablespoons unsalted butter

1 large onion (about 12 ounces), chopped

4 large ribs celery, chopped

1 tablespoon fresh thyme leaves

2 tablespoons minced fresh sage

⅛ teaspoon cayenne

⅔ cup minced fresh parsley

2 large eggs, lightly beaten

½ cup Chicken Stock (page 161) or canned low-sodium chicken broth

1 pint shucked small oysters, with their liquor

CRACKED-PEPPER CORN BREAD

Preheat the oven to 425°F. Coat a 10-inch cast-iron skillet or an 8-inch square baking pan with the cooking spray.

In a large bowl, combine the flour, cornmeal, salt, sugar, baking soda, and cracked peppercorns. In a small bowl, whisk the eggs and buttermilk together until blended; then add to the dry ingredients. Stir in the bacon fat or butter. Pour the batter into the prepared pan, and smooth the top with a rubber spatula.

Bake until the corn bread is golden brown and a toothpick inserted in the center comes out clean, about 25 minutes. Let cool in the pan for 10 minutes; then turn out onto a wire rack to cool completely.

MAKES 1 PAN OF CORN BREAD, ENOUGH FOR 8 CUPS OF CUBES

CRACKED-PEPPER CORN BREAD

Vegetable-oil cooking spray

1	cup all-purpose flour
1	cup yellow cornmeal
1½	teaspoons salt
1	tablespoon sugar
1½	teaspoons baking soda
2	teaspoons coarsely cracked black peppercorns (see Cook's Note)
2	large eggs
1	cup buttermilk
3	tablespoons rendered bacon fat or butter, melted

COOK'S NOTE

If your pepper mill can be adjusted to produce fine to coarse granules, then set it on the coarsest grind. Otherwise, crush the peppercorns using a mortar and pestle or a spice grinder. If you do not have either of these kitchen tools, then place the peppercorns in a heavy lock-top plastic bag, seal the bag, pressing out all the air, and crush the peppercorns with the bottom of a small, heavy saucepan.

WALNUT ROLLS

Homemade rolls may seem a bit ambitious for Thanksgiving dinner, and perhaps they are, but if you love to bake bread, then the work becomes a labor of love. Rolls are a perfect choice if you are only responsible for bringing one or two dishes to the holiday gathering. These are crusty, and every bite is packed with toasted walnuts.

An easy and clever strategy is to start the rolls the day before you want to serve them. After the first rising, place the dough in a gallon-size lock-top plastic bag and refrigerate it overnight. In the morning, complete the second rising; then shape and bake the rolls.

TO MAKE THE SPONGE

In a large bowl, mix together the water, yeast, and sugar. Let stand until it looks creamy and the yeast is activated, about 3 minutes. Stir in the flour, cover loosely with plastic wrap, and let stand in a warm place until bubbly, about 1 hour.

In the meantime, preheat the oven to 350°F. Place the walnuts on a rimmed baking sheet and bake until lightly browned, about 10 minutes. Set aside to cool.

> > >

MAKES **16** ROLLS

SPONGE

1	cup lukewarm (80°F) water
1	teaspoon active dry yeast
¼	teaspoon sugar
1	cup whole wheat flour
2½	cups (10 ounces) chopped walnuts

DOUGH

1	cup lukewarm (80°F) water
1½	teaspoons active dry yeast
1	tablespoon salt
2	tablespoons honey
½	cup walnut oil (see Cook's Note)
1½	teaspoons coarsely ground pepper
4	cups all-purpose flour, plus additional for kneading

TO MAKE THE DOUGH

Stir the walnuts, water, yeast, salt, honey, walnut oil, and pepper into the sponge. Add the flour and stir well with a wooden spoon. If needed, stir in up to ½ cup more flour to make a slightly sticky dough. Turn the dough out on a lightly floured work surface and knead the dough until smooth and elastic, about 5 minutes. Add additional flour only if the dough is sticking. Place the dough back in the bowl, cover with plastic wrap, and let rise in a warm place until doubled in bulk, 1 to 2 hours. (At this point, if making the dough ahead, punch down the dough and place it in a gallon-size lock-top plastic bag. Press out all the air, seal the bag, and refrigerate up to 24 hours. Allow the dough to come to room temperature and rise until double in bulk before proceeding. This will take about 2 hours.)

On a floured work surface, deflate the dough. Using a rolling pin, roll out the dough until it is about ¾ inch thick, using as little flour as necessary to keep the dough from sticking to the work surface or rolling pin. Use a knife to cut the dough into 16 equal pieces. Shape each one into a ball. Place the rolls on nonstick or parchment-lined baking sheets. Cover with a clean dishtowel (do not use a terry towel) or oiled plastic wrap and let rise for 30 minutes.

Fifteen minutes before baking the rolls, preheat the oven to 450°F. Just before baking, use a very sharp serrated knife or a razor metal blade to cut a single slash about 2 inches long in the top of each roll. Place the rolls in the oven, and either spritz the oven walls with water using a spray bottle, or toss 6 ice cubes onto the oven floor, and quickly close the door. Bake for 10 minutes. Spray the oven walls again, or toss 6 more ice cubes onto the oven floor, reduce the temperature to 400°F, and bake 10 minutes longer. Spray the walls again, or toss in more ice cubes, and bake until the rolls are nicely browned, about 10 to 12 minutes.

Transfer to a rack to cool. Serve the rolls at room temperature, or rewarm before serving.

COOK'S NOTE

Walnut oil has a lovely nutty flavor and aroma. It is typically sold in specialty food shops and must be refrigerated once opened. Use it in salad dressings, pasta sauces, and in other baked goods.

HERBED
BUTTERMILK BISCUITS

Biscuits are always a welcome addition to the Thanksgiving table. For those intimidated by yeast dough, biscuits are a great way to show off some baking skills. Plus, you don't need special equipment. Any old baking sheet will do, and if you don't have a biscuit cutter, you can use the rim of a drinking glass or just make drop biscuits. Fresh herbs and the tangy buttermilk make these biscuits especially wonderful.

Preheat the oven to 425°F. In a large bowl, combine the flour, salt, baking soda, baking powder, and pepper. Scatter the butter over the top. Using a pastry cutter or your fingertips, work the butter into the flour until the butter pieces are no larger than peas. Add the herbs and buttermilk, stirring just to blend well. Turn the dough out onto a lightly floured work surface; then, using your fingertips, press the dough into a circle about 1/2 inch thick. Cut 2-inch rounds with a biscuit cutter or use the rim of a drinking glass. Reshape any remaining dough and cut more biscuits. Place the rounds on an ungreased baking sheet.

Brush the biscuits with olive oil. Bake until golden brown, about 18 to 20 minutes. Serve warm, or rewarm just before serving.

2	cups all-purpose flour
3/4	teaspoon salt
1	teaspoon baking soda
1	tablespoon baking powder
1/4	teaspoon freshly ground pepper
4	tablespoons ice-cold unsalted butter, cut into small pieces
2	tablespoons minced fresh parsley
1	tablespoon fresh thyme
1	tablespoon fresh sage
3/4	cup plus 2 tablespoons buttermilk
1 1/2	tablespoons olive oil for brushing

COOK'S NOTE

Of course, biscuits straight from the oven are the ideal, but that gets complicated on Thanksgiving Day. Here are some do-ahead options: Make the biscuits early in the day and rewarm them just before serving. Or make the dough, cut the biscuits, place them on a baking sheet, and cover and refrigerate; then bake just before serving. You can also make the biscuits a couple days ahead, underbake them a bit, and freeze them. Then, without thawing them, finish baking to heat them through.

MINIATURE
MUFFINS WITH
RICOTTA,
CURRANTS, AND DILL

These pretty, dill-specked muffins are a delightful addition to the holiday menu. A basketful of warm muffins wrapped in a crisp linen cloth will delight children and adults alike. I prefer to make miniature muffins, rather than the regular size, because there is *always* room on the edge of a very full Thanksgiving plate for just one little muffin! Make these year-round—they are perfect with an Easter ham or for a Sunday brunch.

Miniature muffin pans are great to have on hand. Use them to make 24 little muffins from any recipe that makes 12 regular ones. These pans are also perfect for little desserts such as pecan or chocolate tartlets, and miniature cheesecakes.

Preheat the oven to 350°F. Coat 24 miniature muffin cups with the cooking spray.

In a small bowl, combine the butter and currants. Set aside. In a medium bowl, mix the flour, cornmeal, sugar, baking powder, and salt. Combine the ricotta, egg, and dill in a small bowl. Pour the cheese mixture over the dry ingredients and fold in, using a rubber spatula, just until the dry ingredients are incorporated. Fold in the butter and currants, just until combined.

Spoon the batter into prepared muffin cups, dividing it evenly among them. Bake until golden brown and a toothpick inserted into the center comes out clean, about 20 minutes. Cool the muffins in the pan set on a rack for 5 minutes. Turn them out and serve hot, or cool on a rack.

MAKES **24** MINIATURE MUFFINS
(OR **12** REGULAR ONES)

Vegetable-oil cooking spray

4 tablespoons unsalted butter, melted

½ cup currants

1¼ cups all-purpose flour

¼ cup yellow cornmeal

⅓ cup sugar

2 teaspoons baking powder

½ teaspoon salt

1 cup ricotta cheese

1 large egg, lightly beaten

3 tablespoons minced fresh dill

SIDE

DISHES

CHAPTER 5

CARAMELIZED
SWEET
POTATO WEDGES

Forgive me. I know this is the sweet potato recipe that is supposed to have miniature marshmallows melted on top, but I can't bring myself to write such a recipe because I don't like the sticky-sweet topping. Many do; it's one of those fond childhood taste memories. I just happen to be one of the loyal opposition. The combination of sweet potatoes and marshmallows goes back to the 1920s, when Florence Taft Eaton published a recipe called Sweet Potatoes de Luxe in *Good Housekeeping*. Though she didn't create the recipe for Thanksgiving, over time, the tradition evolved. If a marshmallow topping is part of your Thanksgiving tradition, then see the Cook's Note for directions.

Set a rack in the center of the oven and a second rack in the upper third. Preheat the oven to 400°F. Coat a 9-by-13-inch baking pan with 1 tablespoon of the butter. Put the sweet potatoes in a large mixing bowl.

In a small saucepan, melt the remaining 4 tablespoons of butter over medium heat. Add ¼ cup of water, the brown sugar, cinnamon, nutmeg, ginger, and salt. Bring to a simmer, stirring constantly, and cook just until the sugar has dissolved. Pour evenly over the potatoes and toss to coat well.

Arrange the sweet potatoes in the prepared baking pan, and cover the dish tightly with foil. Bake in the center of the oven until the sweet potatoes are tender when pierced with a fork, about 45 minutes. Uncover, raise the oven temperature to 475°F, and baste the sweet potatoes. Bake them in the upper third of the oven until the syrup thickens and the potatoes caramelize at the edges, about 20 minutes longer. Serve immediately, or keep warm in a low oven for up to 30 minutes. Baste just before serving.

SERVES 8~10

5	tablespoons unsalted butter
4	large dark-orange-fleshed sweet potatoes (probably labeled "yams"; about 4 pounds total), peeled, cut crosswise in half, and cut then into ½-inch wedges (see page 19)
¾	cup packed dark brown sugar
1½	teaspoons ground cinnamon
½	teaspoon freshly ground nutmeg
⅛	teaspoon ground ginger
1	teaspoon salt

COOK'S NOTE

For the marshmallow variations, you'll need 2 to 2½ cups (about 5 ounces) of miniature marshmallows. Just before serving, spread the marshmallows on top of the sweet potatoes. Broil until the marshmallows are lightly browned, about 2 minutes. Serve immediately.

MAPLE-GLAZED
APPLE
AND SWEET POTATO
GRATIN

SERVES 8~10

The natural affinity between sweet potatoes and maple syrup is highlighted in this elegant side dish. The apple slices add their own sweetness along with a lovely contrasting color to the potatoes. Instead of using an oblong pan, try an 11-inch round shallow casserole or gratin dish, and arrange the sweet potato and apple slices in overlapping concentric circles.

Preheat the oven to 350°F. Coat a 9-by-13-inch baking pan with 1 tablespoon of the butter. Set aside.

In a small saucepan, melt the remaining 4 tablespoons of butter over medium-low heat. Add the flour to the pan, whisking constantly, until the flour is blended and cooked through, about 1 minute. Add the maple syrup, salt, and brown sugar. Simmer, whisking frequently, until the sugar dissolves and the sauce thickens, about 4 minutes. Remove from the heat and reserve.

TO ASSEMBLE THE GRATIN

Arrange a row of alternating sweet potato and apple slices along one side of the pan, overlapping the slices neatly. Arrange additional rows to fill the pan. Pour the reserved sauce evenly on top. Cover the dish tightly with foil and bake for 40 minutes.

Uncover, raise the oven temperature to 450°F, and baste the sweet potatoes and apples with the juices that collect in the bottom of the pan. Bake the gratin, basting every 10 minutes, until the sweet potatoes are tender and nicely browned at the edges, about 30 minutes longer. Serve immediately, or keep warm in a low oven for up to 30 minutes. Baste just before serving. (The gratin can be made up to 8 hours ahead. Cover, and set aside at room temperature until ready to bake.)

5	tablespoons unsalted butter
3	tablespoons all-purpose flour
¾	cup pure maple syrup
½	teaspoon salt
¼	cup packed dark brown sugar
3	large dark-orange-fleshed sweet potatoes (probably labeled "yams"; about 3 pounds total), peeled, and cut into ¼-inch-thick rounds (see page 19)
3	Granny Smith apples (about 1½ pounds total), peeled, cored, and thinly sliced

PUMPKIN VOTIVE

These are festive and colorful votives for the table.

Look for miniature pumpkins that are firm and blemish free.
Cut off the stem and place the votive candle in the top center
of the pumpkin. Use a pencil to outline the base of the votive onto
the pumpkin. Carefully cut out the circle. Use a spoon to scoop
out the pulp. Secure the votive in place.

6 to 8 miniature pumpkins

Razor knife or sharp paring knife

6 to 8 votive candles

Pencil

Spoon

PRALINE
SWEET POTATO
CASEROLE

Forget about leftovers when it comes to this casserole—there never are any. The children sneak back for seconds, and some adults even sneak back for thirds. It's that good. My husband, the dishwasher in the family, can be found scraping leftover caramelized, crusty bits of topping from the pan before he puts it in the sink to soak.

Preheat the oven to 350°F. Pierce each potato several times with a fork and place in a baking pan. Bake until the potatoes are tender when pierced with a fork, 1 1/4 to 1 1/2 hours. Set aside until cool enough to handle.

In a small saucepan, heat the milk and butter until the butter has melted and the mixture is hot but not boiling. Cut the potatoes in half, and scoop the flesh into a large bowl, discarding the skins. Use a potato masher, ricer, or food mill to mash the potatoes. Stir the milk mixture into the potatoes. Whisk in the eggs and continue whisking until well combined with the potato mixture. Add the brown sugar and stir until thoroughly blended. Butter a 9-by-13-inch baking pan, or an 11-inch round oven-to-table casserole. Spread the sweet potato mixture evenly in the casserole. Set aside while making the topping. Increase the oven temperature to 375°F.

TO MAKE THE PRALINE TOPPING
Melt the butter in a 2-quart saucepan over low heat. Stir in the brown sugar, salt, cinnamon, nutmeg, cream, and pecans. Heat to a simmer, and cook, stirring constantly, until the sugar has dissolved and the mixture is thick, about 5 minutes. If the mixture begins to boil and splatter turn down the heat to maintain a simmer. Remove from the heat and stir in the vanilla. Pour the topping evenly over the sweet potatoes, spreading it with a rubber spatula.

Bake the casserole until the topping is slightly crusty and set, about 30 minutes. Serve immediately.

SERVES 8~10

6	large dark-orange-fleshed sweet potatoes (probably labeled "yams"; about 5 1/2 pounds), scrubbed (see page 19)
3/4	cup milk
1/2	cup (1 stick) unsalted butter
3	large eggs, lightly beaten
3/4	cup packed dark brown sugar

PRALINE TOPPING

4	tablespoons unsalted butter
3/4	cup packed dark brown sugar
1/2	teaspoon salt
1/2	teaspoon ground cinnamon
1/2	teaspoon freshly grated nutmeg
3/4	cup heavy (whipping) cream
1 1/2	cups pecans, coarsely chopped
2	teaspoons vanilla

PURÉE OF
YUKON GOLD POTATOES

SERVES 8

Deliciously different from mashed russet potatoes, mashed Yukon golds are creamy rich with a buttery texture and lovely golden hue. Because they have a higher moisture content and are lower in starch than the mealy, russet potato, they require a different proportion of milk and butter when puréed. Be sure to have plenty of gravy on hand; your guests will be ladling gravy over the potatoes as well as the stuffing.

Peel the potatoes and rinse under cold water. Cut each into quarters and place in a 3- to 4-quart saucepan. Cover with cold water, partially cover the pot, and bring the water to a boil. Uncover, add the 1 teaspoon of salt, and reduce the heat so the water boils gently. Cook until the potatoes are tender when pierced with a fork, about 10 to 12 minutes. Meanwhile, in a small saucepan, heat the milk, cream, and butter together until the butter has melted and the mixture is hot but not boiling.

Drain the potatoes and return to the warm pan over low heat for 1 minute to evaporate any excess water. Use a potato masher, ricer, or food mill to mash the potatoes. Stir the milk mixture into the potatoes, a little at a time, until the potatoes are as soft and moist as you like them. Add salt and pepper to taste. Serve immediately, or keep warm in the top of a double boiler, or cover and rewarm in a microwave oven.

6 large Yukon gold potatoes (about 2½ pounds total)

1 teaspoon salt

1 cup milk

½ cup heavy (whipping) cream

½ cup (1 stick) unsalted butter

Freshly ground pepper

CLASSIC
MASHED POTATOES

SERVES 8

There is no such thing as too many starchy dishes on the holiday buffet table, right? For many families, Thanksgiving dinner wouldn't be right without mashed potatoes. It seems there is always one family member relegated to the task of whipping them at the last minute—an honorable duty. And there is always someone else leaning over his shoulder making sure he adds a bit more butter. If you want to assign mashed potato duty to a family member, but would like to avoid the last minute chaos in the kitchen, know that it works perfectly well to cook and mash potatoes up to 1 hour in advance. They can be kept warm in the top of a double boiler set over simmering water, or reheated in a microwave oven just before serving. If you use the do-ahead plan, be sure to add an extra pat of butter, or two!

4 large russet potatoes (about 2 pounds total)

1 teaspoon salt

¾ cups milk

6 tablespoons unsalted butter

Freshly ground pepper

Peel the potatoes and rinse under cold water. Cut each into quarters and place in a 3- to 4-quart saucepan. Cover with cold water, partially cover the pot, and bring the water to a boil. Uncover, add the 1 teaspoon of salt, and reduce the heat so that the water boils gently. Cook until the potatoes are tender when pierced with a fork, about 10 to 12 minutes. Meanwhile, in a small saucepan, heat the milk and butter together until the butter has melted and the mixture is hot but not boiling.

Drain the potatoes and return them to the warm pan over low heat for 1 minute to evaporate any excess water. Use a potato masher, ricer, or food mill to mash the potatoes. Stir the milk and butter mixture into the potatoes, a little at a time, until the potatoes are as soft and moist as you like. Add salt and pepper to taste. Serve immediately, or keep warm in the top of a double boiler, or cover and rewarm in a microwave oven.

GRATIN OF
FENNEL AND TOMATO

I can't tell you how many times I've heard guests say, "Fennel? I've never tasted fennel. This is delicious." Whether sautéed, braised, or sliced raw for salads, fennel is always a surprise, and a delight to serve. Sometimes labeled "sweet anise," fennel has a texture similar to celery and a lovely, mild licorice flavor, which is a perfect foil for a rich meal. This gratin dish has been a part of my Thanksgiving buffet for at least 15 years—it's now a tradition for us, and my family would be disappointed to do without it.

In an 8-inch skillet over medium-high heat, toast the bread crumbs, stirring constantly, until golden brown, about 2 minutes. Set aside to cool.

In a 12-inch sauté pan, heat the oil over medium heat, and swirl to coat the pan. Sauté the garlic and onion until soft, but not brown, about 3 minutes. Add the fennel and continue sautéing, stirring frequently, until the fennel has softened and is beginning to brown, about 5 minutes. Add the tomatoes, salt, and season with pepper to taste. Lower the heat to medium-low and cook, stirring frequently, for 5 minutes longer. Transfer to a shallow oven-to-table casserole or gratin dish.

Preheat the oven to 425°F. In a medium bowl, combine the bread crumbs, Parmesan, and lemon zest. Sprinkle evenly over the fennel mixture. (The gratin can be made up to this point 6 to 8 hours ahead. Cover, and set aside at room temperature.)

Bake the gratin until heated through and the topping is crisp, about 20 minutes. Serve immediately.

SERVES 10

¾ cup dried bread crumbs

5 tablespoons olive oil

3 cloves garlic, minced

1 large yellow onion (about 12 ounces), halved, and cut into ¼-inch slices

6 fennel bulbs, trimmed of stalks, halved, cored, and cut into ¼-inch slices

1 can (28 ounces) diced tomatoes, drained

1 teaspoon salt

Freshly ground pepper

¾ cup (3 ounces) grated Parmesan cheese, preferably Parmigiano-Reggiano

Minced zest of 1 lemon

CARROT PUDDING

Here is one vegetable dish that doesn't need any last minute attention from the busy Thanksgiving cook—and that's a blessing! The carrots can be cooked and puréed a couple of days ahead. Assemble the pudding on Thanksgiving Day, set it aside, and then bake it 1 hour before serving. Hot from the oven, the carrot pudding is gloriously puffed, beautifully browned, and pretty on the plate.

TO PREPARE THE CARROTS

Place the carrots in a medium saucepan and add enough cold water to cover by 1 inch. Bring to a boil over high heat; then reduce to a simmer and cook the carrots until tender when pierced with a fork, about 20 minutes. Drain and cool slightly. Purée the carrots in the work bowl of a food processor fitted with the metal blade. Add the lemon juice, process to combine, and then transfer to a small bowl. (The carrots can be made up to 2 days in advance. Cover and refrigerate; then bring to room temperature before making the pudding.)

Preheat the oven to 350°F. Coat a 2-quart soufflé dish with 1 tablespoon of the butter. Set aside. In a medium mixing bowl, combine the remaining 4 tablespoons of butter, the sugar, flour, salt, pepper, cinnamon, and nutmeg. Beat until smooth. Add the onion and puréed carrots, and beat until well blended. Add the milk and eggs, and mix until smooth. Spoon the mixture into the prepared dish.

Bake, uncovered, until the pudding is puffed and lightly browned and the center is firm to the touch, about 50 minutes to 1 hour. Serve immediately. (The pudding can be assembled several hours ahead. Cover and refrigerate; then remove from the refrigerator 1 hour before baking.)

SERVES 8~10

5	large carrots, peeled and cut into 1-inch chunks
2	teaspoons fresh lemon juice
5	tablespoons unsalted butter, at room temperature
¼	cup sugar
1	tablespoon all-purpose flour
1	teaspoon salt
¼	teaspoon freshly ground pepper
¼	teaspoon ground cinnamon
⅛	teaspoon freshly grated nutmeg
2	tablespoons grated yellow onion
1	cup milk
3	large eggs, lightly beaten

CHIFFONADE OF BRUSSELS SPROUTS

WITH DICED BACON AND HAZELNUTS

SERVES 8~10

This recipe is an adaptation of a side dish I was served at the restaurant JohnFrank in San Francisco. Though they look cute, like miniature cabbages, Brussels sprouts have never been a favorite winter vegetable—until now. Usually they are served whole, overcooked, and "under flavored." So when I was served JohnFrank's Brussels sprouts, which had been shredded and sautéed with bacon and hazelnuts, I couldn't wait to get in the kitchen and try to duplicate what I had eaten.

2	pounds Brussels sprouts
3	slices bacon, finely diced
½	cup chopped toasted hazelnuts (see Cook's Note, page 126)
1	teaspoon salt
½	teaspoon freshly ground pepper

Trim the stem end of the Brussels sprouts and remove any yellow or spotted outer leaves. Cut the Brussels sprouts into $\frac{1}{16}$-inch slices, and use your fingertips to separate the slices into shreds. Alternatively, shred the Brussels sprouts using a food processor with the coarse shredding disk attached. Place in a bowl and set aside until ready to sauté.

Heat a 12-inch sauté pan over medium-high heat. Add the bacon and cook until crisp. Using a slotted spoon, transfer the bacon to a paper towel–lined plate. Set aside. Reserve the bacon fat in the pan.

Just before serving, reheat the bacon fat until hot and add the Brussels sprouts to the pan. Sauté until crisp-tender and bright green, about 3 to 5 minutes. Add the bacon, hazelnuts, salt, and pepper, and stir to mix thoroughly. Taste and adjust the seasonings, and serve.

GOLDEN
CREAMED ONIONS

For many families, creamed onions are almost as traditional as turkey on the Thanksgiving table. There are lots of variations; my favorite is the addition of fresh thyme and parsley, not only for a savory taste, but for the visual appeal of flecks of green herbs against the creamy-white sauce and onions.

Fill a large saucepan two-thirds full with water, and bring to a boil. Add the onions and 1 teaspoon of the salt and boil them in their skins until tender, about 8 minutes. Drain and rinse in cold water; then drain again. Cut off the root end and squeeze at the stem end to slip the onions from their skins. Set aside. (The onions can be cooked 1 day in advance. Cover and refrigerate; then bring to room temperature before making the sauce.)

In a small saucepan, heat the half-and-half just until hot. Set aside.

In a 10-inch sauté pan, melt the butter over medium heat. Add the flour and paprika, and stir with a wire whisk until blended, about 1 minute. Add the half-and-half, whisking continuously, until the sauce is smooth and thickened, about 3 minutes. Add the thyme, parsley, and the remaining 1/2 teaspoon salt; stir to blend. Add the onions and heat through. Add the nutmeg and season with pepper to taste. Serve immediately, or cover and set aside for up to 1 hour. Gently reheat just before serving.

2	pounds pearl onions (do not peel; see Cook's Note)
1½	teaspoons salt
1	cup half-and-half
2	tablespoons unsalted butter
1	tablespoon all-purpose flour
1/8	teaspoon paprika
2	teaspoons fresh thyme leaves
1/4	cup minced fresh parsley
	Pinch of freshly grated nutmeg
	Freshly ground pepper

COOK'S NOTE

I prefer to use fresh pearl onions, and most markets have them during the holiday season. However, frozen pearl onions are a reasonable substitute. They are already peeled and blanched. Boil the onions just until tender, but not falling apart; then drain them for the sauce.

SUCCOTASH
OF CORN, CHANTERELLES, ZUCCHINI, AND
SWEET RED PEPPERS

SERVES 10~12

The Narragansett Indians ate succotash of corn and beans cooked in bear fat. They called it "misickquatash." Fortunately, it has evolved over the years into a much more appetizing dish, which is certainly lower in cholesterol! Served on many Thanksgiving tables, especially in New England, succotash is a colorful addition to the plate.

Peel back the green corn husks and the silk and discard. Trim the base of each ear so it is even and flat, and stand the ear upright on its base. Using a sharp knife, cut down between the cob and the kernels to remove the kernels. Reserve the kernels and discard the cobs.

Fill a large saucepan two-thirds full of water and bring to a boil over high heat. Add the corn and simmer for 3 minutes. Drain in a colander, and then rinse under cold water until cool. Drain thoroughly, blot with paper towels, and reserve.

5   fresh ears of corn (see Cook's Notes)

3   tablespoons unsalted butter

2   medium zucchini (about 1 pound total), cut into ½-inch dice

1   large white onion (about 12 ounces), cut into ½-inch dice

2   medium red bell peppers, seeded, deribbed, and cut into ½-inch dice

1   package (10 ounces) frozen lima beans, thawed

8   ounces chanterelle mushrooms, wiped or brushed clean, stems trimmed, and quartered (see Cook's Notes)

½   cup minced fresh parsley

    Salt and freshly ground pepper

In a 12-inch sauté pan, melt the butter over medium-high heat and swirl to coat the pan. Add the zucchini and onion and sauté, stirring frequently, until just beginning to brown at the edges, about 5 minutes. Add the red peppers and sauté 3 minutes longer. Add the lima beans, reserved corn, and mushrooms. Sauté, stirring constantly, until the mushrooms have softened and the mixture is heated through, about 3 minutes. Stir in the parsley, and salt and pepper to taste. Serve immediately, or keep warm for up to 20 minutes.

COOK'S NOTES

Nowadays, with our global markets, fresh corn is available year-round. In November, I don't buy fresh corn to eat it on the cob (I save that eating pleasure for summer, when the corn is local and just-picked fresh). However, I do use November corn in sautés and soups—in fact, I prefer fresh corn to frozen because the texture is tender and firm. The variety of corn available in the markets at this time of year is, most likely, a hybrid known as Super-sweet. As a result of the high sugar content, the corn caramelizes a bit when sautéed, which gives a welcome, rich flavor to the succotash.

Delicate, golden-hued chanterelle mushrooms appear in many markets in the fall. These mushrooms are buttery-rich in flavor and perfume any dish with a fresh, woodsy scent. If you can't find them fresh, dried are available—just soak them in warm water to soften. A reasonable substitute would be fresh shiitake mushrooms or, if need be, cremini mushrooms. Use sautéed chanterelles in omelets, with pasta, or in risotto. For me, they are a seasonal treasure.

PILLAR CANDLES IN AN AUTUMNAL WREATH

Pillar candles set in a wreath made from leaves bring festive candlelight and color to your Thanksgiving table.

Weave the stems of the leaves into the wreath, overlapping the leaves to create fullness. Set on the plate and place the pillar candles in the center.

WREATH TRIVETS
Need extra trivets? Use plain 8-inch grapevine or twig wreaths as a decorative and inexpensive solution.

2 to 3 twig or grapevine wreaths (6 inches in diameter; available at craft stores)

Fresh or naturally preserved fallen leaves (see Note)

Small, flat plate

2 to 3 pillar candles (2½ inches wide)

NOTE
Preserved fallen leaves are available at craft stores. They can be pressed with a cool iron if wrinkled.

CRANBERRY **CHUTNEY**

After making my first batch of cranberry chutney years ago, and the many variations since, I have been hard-pressed to go back to the more traditional cranberry sauce or relish. Though I love cranberries in any form, this chutney with diced pears and apples is jewel-like when served in a glass or cut-crystal bowl. It's a perfect do-ahead recipe, easily transported if Thanksgiving is at someone else's home, and it makes a great gift packed in pint-size glass jars.

In a deep 6-quart saucepan, combine the cranberries, sugar, 1 1/4 cups water, cloves, cinnamon sticks, and salt. Bring to a boil over medium heat, stirring frequently to dissolve the sugar. Cook until the cranberries begin to pop open, about 10 to 12 minutes. Adjust the heat so the mixture simmers. Stir in the apples, pears, onion, raisins, and ginger. Continue to cook, stirring frequently, until thick, 10 to 15 minutes longer. Remove from the heat, stir in the hazelnuts, and allow the mixture to cool to room temperature. Discard the cinnamon sticks and cloves if you can find them. Refrigerate in tightly sealed jars for up to 3 months.

MAKES ABOUT **2** QUARTS

4   cups fresh or frozen cranberries, picked over, and stemmed

2½   cups sugar

6   whole cloves

2   cinnamon sticks, each about 3 inches long

1   teaspoon salt

2   Granny Smith apples (about 6 ounces each), peeled, cored, and cut into ½-inch dice

2   firm Bosc or Anjou pears (about 6 ounces each), peeled, cored, and cut into ½-inch dice

1   small yellow onion (about 5 ounces), diced

1   cup golden raisins

⅓   cup diced crystallized ginger (see Cook's Notes)

½   cup whole hazelnuts, toasted, skins removed, and halved (see Cook's Notes)

COOK'S NOTES

Crystallized ginger slices are typically packaged in 4-ounce boxes and are available in the Asian foods section of well-stocked supermarkets.

Try to buy shelled hazelnuts (also known as "filberts") with the skins removed. To toast, place the nuts on a rimmed baking sheet in a preheated 375°F oven. Toast for about 15 minutes, until lightly browned. If they have skins, when they are cool enough to handle, lay them on a clean kitchen towel, or between several sheets of paper towels. Rub the nuts to remove most of the skins (they never completely come off). You can substitute unsalted cashews, if necessary. Toast like hazelnuts, until lightly browned, about 12 to 15 minutes.

CRANBERRY-ORANGE
RELISH WITH MINT

This is my mother's recipe, to which I have added fresh mint. One of my jobs on Thanksgiving morning was to hold the bowl under the hand-cranked meat grinder, which was attached to the edge of the butcher block counter, while my mother ground the fresh cranberries and orange for relish. Thank goodness for the invention of the food processor! This relish is tart and goes so well with the holiday bird. I like the addition of fresh mint, but the relish is equally good without it.

In the work bowl of a food processor fitted with the metal blade, combine the cranberries, orange, sugar, and salt. Process until coarsely and evenly ground, stopping the machine once or twice to scrape down the sides of the work bowl. Add the mint, and process to combine. Transfer the relish to a serving bowl, cover, and refrigerate for several hours before serving. (The relish can be made 1 or 2 days in advance; however, wait until the day you serve it to add the fresh mint.)

MAKES ABOUT 3 CUPS

1   package (12 ounces) fresh cranberries, picked over, and stemmed

1   small navel orange, including the peel, quartered

½   cup sugar

½   teaspoon salt

2   tablespoons minced fresh mint

CRANBERRY
SALSA WITH LIME

Sukey Garcetti, a friend from Los Angeles, shared some recipes from her family's Mexican Thanksgiving menu. Her husband, Gil, is mostly of Mexican descent (despite his Italian surname) and comes from a family of talented cooks. Reinterpreting salsa, using cranberries instead of tomatoes, is a terrific, nontraditional spin on cranberry sauce. Gil's mother chopped everything by hand. I took the liberty of grinding the cranberries in a food processor, but I prefer the look of the celery, onion, and jalapeño diced by hand.

In the work bowl of a food processor fitted with the metal blade, process the cranberries until coarsely and evenly ground. Transfer to a medium mixing bowl. Add all the remaining ingredients. Stir well to combine. Transfer to a serving bowl, cover, and refrigerate until ready to serve. (The salsa is best if made several hours and up to 1 day in advance to allow the flavors to meld.)

1	package (12 ounces) fresh cranberries, picked over and stemmed
2	large ribs celery, finely diced
1	small white onion (about 4 ounces), finely diced
1	jalapeño chile, seeded and minced (see Cook's Note)
1/4	cup chopped fresh cilantro
1/2	teaspoon salt
3/4	cup sugar
3	tablespoons fresh lime juice

COOK'S NOTE
Keep some disposable surgical gloves on hand (available at any pharmacy) to wear while working with fresh chiles. When oils from cut fresh chiles get on your hands, they can easily irritate your eyes or nose if you touch them.

SAUTÉED
GREEN BEANS WITH
SHALLOT CRISPS

SERVES 8~10

My grandmother never knew I was the culprit; she never caught me red-handed, snitching the canned french-fried onions off the top of the green-bean bake she made every Thanksgiving. But every year, most of those crisp onions disappeared before anyone began filling a plate from the buffet table. That was some thirty-five years ago. Now that I'm at the helm when it comes to cooking Thanksgiving dinner, I've updated that classic recipe.

I still love crisp onions, green beans have always been a favorite vegetable, and the combination is a natural. So, in my pursuit of using fresh vegetables whenever possible, I offer this modern version of the green-bean bake. Keep your eye on the buffet table, though, because these shallot crisps are mighty good.

TO MAKE THE SHALLOT CRISPS
Set a plate lined with a double thickness of paper towels next to the stove. Heat the vegetable oil in a 6-inch sauté pan over medium-high heat until hot but not smoking. (Test the temperature of the oil by adding 1 slice of shallot to the hot oil. If the oil begins to bubble and sizzle without splattering, and the shallot turns golden, then the oil is ready.) Using a slotted spoon, add half of the shallots to the oil. Fry until they are crisp and turn a dark golden brown, about 1 to 2 minutes. Remove from the oil and drain on paper towels. Repeat with the remaining shallots. Set aside at room temperature until ready to garnish the beans. The shallot crisps can be made several hours ahead.

TO SAUTÉ THE BEANS
Heat a 12-inch sauté pan over medium-high heat. Add the butter and olive oil, swirl to coat the pan, and then add the green beans. Sauté, stirring frequently, until the beans are bright green and crisp-tender, about 5 minutes. Season with salt and pepper to taste. Transfer the beans to a warmed serving bowl and garnish with the shallot crisps. Serve immediately.

SHALLOT CRISPS

⅓ cup vegetable oil

½ cup thinly sliced shallots (about 5 to 6 shallots)

2 tablespoons unsalted butter

2 tablespoons olive oil

2 pounds green beans, trimmed

Salt and freshly ground pepper

DESSERTS

CHAPTER 6

PUMPKIN **POUND CAKE**

WITH FRENCH VANILLA
ICE CREAM

This is a luscious, buttery, pumpkin-hued pound cake that, I promise you, will disappear in a hurry. I make mine in a nonstick decorative Bundt pan, sprinkle it with powdered sugar while it is still warm, and serve it on a doily-lined pedestal cake plate. It is picture perfect. A scoop of French vanilla ice cream is a delicious accompaniment.

Position a rack in the lower third of the oven and preheat it to 350°F. Butter a 10-inch tube pan or 12-cup Bundt pan. (Use the non-stick kind, if you have one.) Sift together the flour, baking powder, salt, ginger, nutmeg, cloves, cinnamon, and cardamom. Set aside. Separate the eggs, putting the yolks in a small bowl, and the whites in a large mixing bowl.

In a large bowl, using an electric mixer, cream the butter on medium speed until it is smooth, about 1 minute. Pour the bourbon or vanilla over the brown sugar. Reduce the mixer speed to low, and slowly add the brown sugar, about $1/2$ cup at a time. When all the sugar has been added, stop the mixer, scrape down the sides, and continue to cream the mixture until light and fluffy, about 3 to 4 minutes. Use a fork to lightly beat the egg yolks; then, on low speed, add them to the butter-sugar mixture 1 tablespoon at a time. Scrape down the sides of the bowl, increase the speed to medium, and beat for 1 minute. Add the pumpkin purée and beat on low speed, until smooth.

2½	cups cake flour
1½	teaspoons baking powder
½	teaspoon salt, plus pinch for egg whites
½	teaspoon ground ginger
¼	teaspoon freshly grated nutmeg
¼	teaspoon ground cloves
1½	teaspoons ground cinnamon
¼	teaspoon ground cardamom
4	large eggs, at room temperature
1	cup (2 sticks) unsalted butter, at room temperature
1	tablespoon bourbon whiskey, or 2 teaspoons pure vanilla extract
2	cups lightly packed dark brown sugar
1	cup unsweetened pumpkin purée
¼	cup powdered sugar
1	quart French vanilla ice cream

Using a rubber spatula, stir in one-third of the flour mixture, and continue stirring just until the flour disappears. Do not beat or overmix. Repeat, adding the remaining flour mixture in 2 batches. Scrape down the sides of the bowl, and then set aside.

Add a pinch of salt to the egg whites, and beat using an electric mixer, just until they hold soft peaks. Fold them gently, but thoroughly, into the batter. Spoon the batter into the prepared pan, and spread it around evenly with a rubber spatula. Bake for 45 to 50 minutes, or until a toothpick inserted near the center of the cake comes out clean. Let the cake rest in the pan, set on a rack, for 10 minutes. Place a cooling rack on top of the cake, invert the cake, and then remove the pan. Using a sifter or fine-mesh sieve, sift the powdered sugar over the cake. Cool completely. Cut the cake into ¾-inch-thick slices and serve with a scoop of French vanilla ice cream.

COOK'S NOTE

Store the cake, covered, at room temperature for 1 or 2 days; or freeze, wrapped tightly with plastic wrap, then foil, for up to 2 weeks.

HARVEST TOPIARY

Mix sheaves of dried wheat and rye tied with French ribbon to create a pair of topiaries for your sideboard or holiday table.

Cut 2 pieces of florist foam with a knife into 2½-by-3-inch cubes. Place 1 inside each terra-cotta pot. Mix the dried wheat and rye and divide into 2 bunches 3 to 3½ inches in diameter. Wrap and secure each one with wire about halfway down the sheath, and again about 1 inch from the bottom. Hold a bunch securely and press firmly into the florist foam, making sure it is straight vertically. Fill the pot with mixed nuts, mounding them at the center. Cut the ribbon in half, making two 18-inch-long pieces. Wrap each ribbon around a bunch several times, covering the wire, and tie with a bow.

Florist foam (used for dried arrangements)

Knife

2 (6-inch) terra-cotta pots

2 to 3 large bunches dried wheat

2 to 3 large bunches dried rye

Thin wire (30 gauge)

2 pounds mixed nuts (pecans, walnuts, filberts)

Scissors or wire cutter

1 yard French wire ribbon

DOUBLE-CRUSTED
CRANBERRY-
BLUEBERRY PIE

I have been making this tart, crimson-colored berry pie for as many Thanksgivings as I can remember. My children would be terribly disappointed if it was missing as one of the dessert offerings. In fact, they love it so much, I am certain they lick their plates when I'm not looking. If you live, as I do, in an area where huckleberries grow wild, pick them in late summer and stash some in the freezer for this pie. (Blueberries are delicious in this dish, but huckleberries are even better.)

TO MAKE THE CRUST
Combine the flour, salt, and sugar in a food processor fitted with the metal blade. Add the butter and shortening and pulse until the mixture resembles coarse meal. Add the sour cream and water, and process for a few seconds, just until a ball of dough begins to form. Do not overprocess. (To make the dough by hand, place the dry ingredients in a large bowl, and use a pastry blender to cut the butter and shortening into the flour mixture. Add the sour cream and ice water, and mix just until it comes together and forms a mass.)

Transfer the dough to a floured work surface, gathering all the loose bits, and form into a disk about 1 inch thick. Cut the dough into 2 pieces, wrap each one in plastic wrap, and refrigerate for at least 30 minutes, or overnight.

TO MAKE THE FILLING
Coarsely grind the orange in a food processor or blender. In a large saucepan, combine all the remaining ingredients. Stir to combine, and bring to a boil. Reduce the heat to a simmer, and cook, stirring constantly, until the mixture has thickened and the sugar has dissolved, about 4 minutes. Set aside and cool completely.

> > >

MAKES ONE 10-INCH PIE;
SERVES 8~10

PIE CRUST

2½ cups all-purpose flour, plus extra for dusting

1 teaspoon salt

2 teaspoons sugar

½ cup (1 stick) ice-cold unsalted butter, cut into small pieces

½ cup ice-cold solid vegetable shortening

⅓ cup sour cream

2 tablespoons ice water

FILLING

½ small orange, including peel, seeded and quartered

1 package (12 ounces) fresh or frozen cranberries, picked over and stemmed

4 cups (about 1¼ pounds) fresh or frozen blueberries or huckleberries

½ teaspoon salt

1⅔ cups sugar

3 tablespoons cornstarch

TO ASSEMBLE THE PIE

Position a rack in the center of the oven and place another rack under it. Preheat the oven to 400°F. Have a 10-inch pie pan ready. On a lightly floured work surface, roll out 1 piece of the dough into a circle about 12 inches in diameter. (Dust the work surface and dough with a little more flour, as necessary, to keep the dough from sticking.) Roll the dough around the rolling pin, lift it over the pie pan, and unroll the dough over the pan. Adjust to center the dough; then press it into place.

Roll out the remaining dough into a 12-inch circle. Spoon the cooled filling into the pie shell, mounding it in the center. Using a pastry brush dipped in the milk, moisten the sides of the bottom crust. Drape the top crust over the pie. Lightly press the top and bottom crust edges together. Trim the excess dough by running a knife around the edge of the pan. Crimp the edges to make a decorative border. Cut 3 or 4 slits in the top crust to allow steam to escape. Brush with milk, and sprinkle with the turbinado sugar.

Place the pie in the center of the oven, and place a rimmed baking sheet on the rack below. Bake until the crust is golden brown, about 50 minutes. Cool on a rack. Serve the pie warm or at room temperature.

SUGAR TOPPING

2 tablespoons milk

1 tablespoon turbinado sugar (see Cook's Note) or granulated sugar

COOK'S NOTE

Turbinado sugar is usually available in the baking supplies aisle of a large supermarket. It is light brown and has large crystals. Use it to sprinkle on muffins, scones, and pies just before baking.

SPICED PUMPKIN PIE

WITH PECAN PASTRY CRUST

MAKES TWO 9-INCH PIES;
SERVES 16~20

There is stiff competition out there for the best pumpkin pie recipe. After all, pumpkin pie has been around since the Pilgrims' second Thanksgiving, in 1623. This version is my favorite because I like the contrast between the smooth custard filling and the nutty flavor and crunch of the crust. You can't go wrong if you serve this pumpkin pie with whipped cream.

TO MAKE THE CRUST

Combine the flour, pecans, salt, and sugar in a food processor fitted with the metal blade. Add the butter and shortening, and pulse until the mixture resembles coarse meal. Add the sour cream and water, and process for a few seconds, just until a ball of dough begins to form. Do not overprocess. (To make the dough by hand, place the dry ingredients in a large bowl, and use a pastry blender to cut the butter and shortening into the flour mixture. Add the sour cream and ice water, and mix just until the dough comes together and forms a mass.)

Transfer the dough to a floured work surface, gathering all the loose bits, and form into a disk about 1 inch thick. Cut the dough into 2 pieces, wrap each piece in plastic wrap, and refrigerate for at least 30 minutes, or overnight.

Have two 9-inch pie pans ready. On a lightly floured work surface, roll out 1 piece of the dough into a circle about 12 inches in diameter. Dust the work surface and dough with a little more flour, as necessary, to keep the dough from sticking. Roll the dough around the rolling pin, lift it over the pie pan, and unroll the dough over the pan. Adjust to center the dough; then press it into place. Trim the excess dough by running a knife around the edge of the pan. Set it aside, leaving it rolled out. Repeat with the second piece of dough. Refrigerate the pie crusts while you make the decorative edge pieces.

> > >

PIE CRUST

2¼ cups all-purpose flour, plus extra for dusting

½ cup finely ground pecans, toasted (see Cook's Note)

1 teaspoon salt

1 tablespoon sugar

½ cup (1 stick) ice-cold unsalted butter, cut into small pieces

½ cup ice-cold solid vegetable shortening

⅓ cup sour cream

2 tablespoons ice water

COOK'S NOTES

Toasting nuts brings out their full, rich flavor. Place the nuts in a single layer on a rimmed baking sheet and bake in a preheated 350°F oven until lightly browned, about 10 minutes. Alternatively, the nuts can be browned in a microwave. Place in a single layer on a microwave-safe plate, and microwave on high power for 2 to 3 minutes, or until lightly browned. Watch carefully that they don't burn.

If you prefer to crimp the edges of the pumpkin pies rather than make decorative cutouts, then instead of trimming the pastry to the edge of the pan, leave about 1 inch of overhanging dough. Turn it under, and crimp the edges to make a decorative border.

Use a 1¼-inch decorative cookie cutter (such as a leaf, daisy, or star shape) to make cutouts from the dough trimmings. Reroll the scraps to make more cutouts. You should have about 30 to 35 dough shapes per pie. Place in a single layer on a nonstick baking sheet and refrigerate.

TO MAKE THE FILLING

In a large mixing bowl, combine the pumpkin, eggs, molasses, sugar, salt, ginger, cinnamon, allspice, nutmeg, and pepper. Whisk until smooth. Blend in the sour cream and heavy cream. Whisk until smooth and no white streaks are visible. Set aside.

TO ASSEMBLE THE PIES

Position a rack in the center of the oven. Preheat the oven to 350°F. Divide the pumpkin filling between the two chilled pie shells. Use a pastry brush to brush milk along the edge of the pastry. Overlap the decorative cutouts around the edge of the pastry, pressing gently. There should be enough to circle each pan. Brush with milk and sprinkle with sugar. Bake the pies until the filling just begins to puff at the edges and the center no longer jiggles when gently shaken, about 45 to 50 minutes. Cool completely.

TO MAKE THE TOPPING

Combine the cream, powdered sugar, and rum or maple syrup in a medium bowl. Use a whisk or electric mixer to whip the cream until soft peaks form. Cover and refrigerate until ready to serve.

Slice the pies into wedges, top with whipped cream, and serve.

FILLING

3½ cups or 2 cans (15 ounces each) unsweetened pumpkin purée

7 large eggs, lightly beaten

⅔ cup unsulphured molasses

⅓ cup sugar

½ teaspoon salt

1 tablespoon ground ginger

1 tablespoon ground cinnamon

½ teaspoon ground allspice

1 teaspoon freshly grated nutmeg

½ teaspoon freshly ground pepper

2 cups sour cream

1 cup heavy (whipping) cream

2 tablespoons milk

Sugar for sprinkling

TOPPING

1 cup heavy (whipping) cream

2 tablespoons powdered sugar

2 tablespoons dark rum,
or 1 tablespoon pure maple syrup

HOLLYE'S **PECAN PIE**
WITH **SPIKED** CHANTILLY CREAM

MAKES ONE 9- OR 10-INCH PIE;
SERVES 8~10

Hollye Maxwell, an artist friend of mine, grew up in Acworth, Georgia, a small town about thirty-five miles north of Atlanta. Although she now lives in Portland, Oregon, she hasn't lost her delightful accent, her penchant for saying "Yes, ma'am," or her love for pecan pie. Her family had pecan trees on their property. Her father invented a gizmo for picking up pecans from the ground without bending over, and her mother made this pie. It's simply the best pecan pie I've ever tasted. Pecan pies are too often sickeningly sweet. The secret here is brown rice syrup, which is readily available in natural food stores.

TO MAKE THE CRUST
Combine the flour, salt, and sugar in a food processor fitted with the metal blade. Add the butter and shortening and pulse until the mixture resembles coarse meal. Add the sour cream and water, and process for a few seconds, just until a ball of dough begins to form. Do not overprocess. (To make the dough by hand, place the dry ingredients in a large bowl, and use a pastry blender to cut the butter and shortening into the flour mixture. Add the sour cream and ice water, and mix just until it comes together and forms a mass.)

Transfer the dough to a floured work surface, gathering all the loose bits, and form into a disk about 1 inch thick. Wrap the dough in plastic wrap, and refrigerate for at least 30 minutes, or overnight.

> > >

PIE CRUST

1¼ cups all-purpose flour, plus extra for dusting

½ teaspoon salt

2 teaspoons sugar

4 tablespoons ice-cold unsalted butter, cut into small pieces

¼ cup ice-cold solid vegetable shortening

3 tablespoons sour cream

1 tablespoon ice water

Have a 9- or 10-inch pie pan ready. On a lightly floured work surface, roll out the dough into a circle about 12 inches in diameter. Dust the work surface and dough with a little more flour, as necessary, to keep the dough from sticking. Roll the dough around the rolling pin, lift it over the pie pan, and unroll the dough over the pan. Adjust to center the dough; then press it into place. Trim the excess dough, leaving a $1/2$-inch overhang; then tuck it under itself to form a double thickness around the edge of the pan. Crimp the edges with a fork, or use your fingers to flute the edges to form a decorative pie crust. Refrigerate the crust while you make the filling. Position a rack in the center of the oven and preheat the oven to 400°F.

TO MAKE THE FILLING
In a large mixing bowl, combine the eggs, brown rice syrup, maple syrup, vanilla, melted butter, and salt. Whisk until smooth. Fold in the pecans, and set aside.

TO ASSEMBLE THE PIE
Pour the pecan filling into the chilled pie shell. Use a pastry brush to brush some of the milk along the edge of the pastry. Place the pie in the oven, and immediately reduce the temperature to 350°F. Bake the pie until the filling just begins to puff at the edges and the center no longer jiggles when gently shaken, about 40 to 45 minutes. Cool completely.

TO MAKE THE TOPPING
Combine the cream, powdered sugar, and bourbon whiskey in a medium bowl. Use a whisk or electric mixer to whip the cream until soft peaks form. Cover and refrigerate until ready to serve.

Slice the pie into wedges, top with whipped cream, and serve.

FILLING

3	large eggs, lightly beaten
1	cup brown rice syrup (see Cook's Note)
¼	cup pure maple syrup
1	teaspoon pure vanilla extract
3	tablespoons unsalted butter, melted
⅛	teaspoon salt
2	cups pecan halves
1	tablespoon milk

CHANTILLY CREAM

1	cup heavy (whipping) cream
2	tablespoons powdered sugar
1	tablespoon bourbon whiskey

COOK'S NOTE
Brown rice syrup is a sweetener. Light brown in color, it is only moderately sweet in comparison with corn syrup. For those with wheat allergies, it has the advantage of being gluten-free. Brown rice syrup is typically sold in glass jars, and is found in the baking section of natural food stores.

CHOCOLATE GINGERBREAD WITH
SUGAR-GLAZED APPLES

When we wrote *The Basic Gourmet* cookbook in 1995, my coauthor, Dan Taggart, developed a wonderfully moist, spicy chocolate gingerbread. I've made this easy, freeze-ahead dessert for several Thanksgivings since then. It's perfect cut into squares and presented alongside a pie or tart on the dessert buffet. Accompany the gingerbread with warm sugar-glazed apple wedges as an alternative to the traditional dollop of whipped cream.

TO MAKE THE GINGERBREAD

Position a rack in the lower third of the oven and preheat to 350°F. Coat a 9-by-13-inch baking pan with the cooking spray. Shake 2 tablespoons of flour over the bottom and sides of the pan, tilting to coat all sides. Turn the pan upside down over a sink, and tap the sides and bottom to remove the excess flour.

Over a small bowl, sift together the 2½ cups of flour, the baking soda, baking powder, salt, ginger, and cinnamon. Set aside.

In a 2½-quart saucepan over medium-low heat, combine the coffee, chocolate, and butter. Stir until the butter and chocolate have melted; then remove from the heat. Stir in the molasses, brown sugar, and eggs. Transfer this mixture to a large mixing bowl.

Using a large rubber spatula, stir the flour mixture into the wet ingredients in the large bowl, mixing just until the flour is absorbed. Pour into the prepared pan. Bake until a toothpick or cake tester inserted in the center of the cake comes out clean, about 45 minutes. Cool in the pan on a wire cake rack. (The cake can be made 2 days ahead, covered with plastic wrap, and stored at room temperature. It also freezes well. Freeze it in the pan, tightly covered, for up to 1 month. Thaw at room temperature before serving.)

> > >

GINGERBREAD

Vegetable-oil cooking spray

2½ cups, plus 2 tablespoons all-purpose flour

1 teaspoon baking soda

1 teaspoon baking powder

½ teaspoon salt

2 teaspoons ground ginger

1½ teaspoons ground cinnamon

1½ cups brewed coffee (see Cook's Note)

2 ounces unsweetened baking chocolate

½ cup (1 stick) unsalted butter

1 cup dark molasses

1 cup lightly packed dark brown sugar

2 large eggs, lightly beaten

TO MAKE THE APPLES

Melt the butter in a 12-inch sauté pan over medium-high heat. Add the apple wedges, toss to coat with the butter, and sauté for 1 minute. Sprinkle the apples with the sugar, stirring constantly, and sauté until lightly browned but still crisp, about 4 to 5 minutes. Remove the pan from the heat and set aside. Rewarm just before serving. (The apples can be sautéed up to 2 hours ahead.)

SUGAR-GLAZED APPLES

3 tablespoons unsalted butter

4 underripe Golden Delicious apples, peeled, cored, and cut into ½-inch wedges

¼ cup sugar

COOK'S NOTE

Coffee to be used in baking may be freshly brewed or made with instant powder or granules stirred into hot water.

BOSC PEAR
AND TOASTED HAZELNUT
TART

A tart makes such a pretty presentation on a dessert table,
especially this one, which has slices of caramelized pears on top.
The skin of a Bosc pear is autumn-hued in lovely shades of brown
and gold, which is precisely why the pears are left unpeeled.
The tart can be made in stages: the crust can be prepared in
advance and frozen, and the filling can be made 1 day ahead.
This makes assembly and baking on Thanksgiving Day a breeze.

TO MAKE THE CRUST

Combine the hazelnuts, flour, salt, and sugar in a food processor
fitted with the metal blade. Add the butter and shortening and
pulse until the mixture resembles coarse meal. Add the sour cream
and water, and process for a few seconds, just until a ball of
dough begins to form. Do not overprocess. (To make the dough by
hand, place the dry ingredients in a large bowl, and use a pastry
blender to cut the butter and shortening into the flour mixture.
Add the sour cream and ice water, and mix just until it comes
together and forms a mass.)

Transfer the dough to a floured work surface, gathering all the
loose bits, and form into a disk about 1 inch thick. Wrap the
dough in plastic wrap, and refrigerate for at least 30 minutes,
or overnight.

Preheat the oven to 425°F. Have ready a 10-inch tart pan with a
removable bottom. On a lightly floured work surface, roll out the
dough into a circle about 12 inches in diameter. Dust the work
surface and dough with a little more flour, as necessary, to keep
the dough from sticking. Roll the dough around the rolling pin, lift
it over the tart pan, and unroll the dough over the pan. Adjust to
center the dough; then press it into place. Trim the overhang to
1/2 inch and fold in to reinforce the side. Freeze the tart shell for
20 minutes. (The tart shell can be made up to this point and frozen
for up to 1 month.)

> > >

TART CRUST

1/4	cup finely ground toasted hazelnuts (see Cook's Note)
1 1/4	cups all-purpose flour, plus extra for dusting
1/2	teaspoon salt
2	teaspoons sugar
4	tablespoons ice-cold unsalted butter, cut into small pieces
1/4	cup ice-cold solid vegetable shortening
3	tablespoons sour cream
1	tablespoon ice water

Line the tart shell with foil and fill with dried beans, rice, or pie weights. Bake just until the side of the pastry begins to color, about 20 minutes. Remove the weights and foil, and bake until the base of the shell is golden, about 5 minutes. Transfer to a rack to cool. Reduce the oven temperature to 400°F.

TO MAKE THE FILLING

Cream the butter and sugar in a food processor fitted with the metal blade, stopping the machine once or twice to scrape down the sides of the work bowl. Add the egg yolk, egg, and heavy cream, and process to blend thoroughly. Scatter the ground nuts and flour over the butter mixture, and process just until blended. Refrigerate while preparing the pears. Halve and core them and cut lengthwise into $1/8$-inch slices.

TO ASSEMBLE THE TART

Spread the cream filling evenly over the bottom of the prepared tart shell. Arrange the pears over the filling in overlapping concentric circles, starting from the outside edge and working toward the center. Brush the pears with the pear brandy. Sprinkle the $1\frac{1}{2}$ tablespoons of sugar over the top.

Bake the tart in the center of the oven until the pastry is brown and the pears begin to caramelize, about 45 minutes. Let cool on a rack. When ready to serve, center one hand under the bottom of the tart pan and slip off the rim with the other hand. Set the tart on a round serving plate and cut into wedges.

FILLING

$\frac{1}{2}$	cup (1 stick) unsalted butter, cut into small pieces
$\frac{1}{2}$	cup sugar
1	large egg yolk
1	large egg
1	tablespoon heavy (whipping) cream
$\frac{1}{2}$	cup finely ground hazelnuts (see Cook's Note)
1	tablespoon all-purpose flour
3	firm but ripe Bosc pears
2	tablespoons pear brandy, kirsch, or Cognac
$1\frac{1}{2}$	tablespoons sugar

COOK'S NOTE

Prepare the ground hazelnuts for both the tart shell and filling at the same time. Spread 1 cup of hazelnuts on a rimmed baking sheet and toast them in a preheated 350°F oven until lightly browned, about 10 minutes. Rub the nuts together in a terry kitchen towel to remove the skins. (Not all of the skins will come off, and that is not a problem.) Place them in a food processor fitted with the metal blade and process until finely ground. Measure and set aside ¼ cup for the tart shell and ½ cup for the filling.

PUMPKIN
CHEESECAKE WITH A
GINGERSNAP CRUMB CRUST

MAKES ONE 9- OR 10-INCH CHEESE-
CAKE; SERVES 10~12

As if the Thanksgiving meal weren't rich enough! But who cares? This cheesecake is so divinely smooth and creamy that even a little sliver is satisfying. The filling is rich with pumpkin flavor and sweet spices, which pair perfectly with the gingersnap crust. I have to admit, this cheesecake is a favorite leftover for breakfast—it's perfect with a morning cup of coffee. Unlike a pumpkin pie, this dessert can be made a couple days in advance, or even frozen for up to 1 month.

Preheat the oven to 375°F. Butter a 9- or 10-inch springform pan with 1 tablespoon of the melted butter. In a medium bowl, combine the gingersnap crumbs with the remaining ⅓ cup of butter until thoroughly blended. Press the crumbs into the bottom and about 1 inch up the side of the prepared pan. Bake the crust until crisp and lightly colored, about 10 to 12 minutes. Cool on a rack. Reduce the oven temperature to 350°F.

In the work bowl of a food processor fitted with the metal blade, process the cream cheese until smooth. Mix in both sugars, then the eggs, and continue processing until the mixture is thoroughly combined, scraping down the side of the bowl once or twice. Add the cinnamon, nutmeg, ginger, vanilla, pumpkin purée, and sour cream. Process until completely smooth and all ingredients are thoroughly combined. (Alternatively, beat the ingredients in a large bowl using an electric mixer.)

Gently pour the cheesecake filling into the prebaked crust. The filling will likely rise above the crust, which is not a problem. Place the cheesecake in the center of the oven and bake until the sides are slightly puffed, about 35 to 40 minutes. The center of the filling will still be very soft and will jiggle when you shake the pan gently. Turn off the oven and leave the cheesecake in the oven, undisturbed, for 1 hour. Transfer it to a rack and let cool in the pan. Cover and refrigerate for at least 6 hours, but preferably overnight. (The cheesecake can also be wrapped tightly and frozen for up to 1 month. Allow to thaw 12 hours in the refrigerator.)

To serve, unlatch the rim of the pan and carefully remove. Cut slices with a warm, wet knife, wiping the knife clean between slices.

⅓	cup, plus 1 tablespoon unsalted butter, melted
2	cups gingersnap crumbs (about 8 ounces of cookies; see Cook's Note)
3	packages (8 ounces each) cream cheese, softened
½	cup granulated sugar
½	cup light brown sugar
3	large eggs, lightly beaten
1	teaspoon ground cinnamon
½	teaspoon freshly grated nutmeg
½	teaspoon ground ginger
1	tablespoon pure vanilla extract
1	can (15 ounces) unsweetened pumpkin purée
¼	cup sour cream

COOK'S NOTE

Use store-bought gingersnap cookies labeled "old-fashioned" and packaged in a 1-pound box. To make finely ground crumbs, grind the cookies in 2 batches, using a food processor or blender.

RUSTIC
APPLE ALMOND TART

A free-form tart, whether it's called a *galette* in French or a *crostata* in Italian, is a boon to a novice dessert maker. The dough is rolled out, a fruit filling is mounded in the center, and the edges are folded over the filling. There's no fitting the dough into a pie plate and crimping the edges, which can be intimidating to say the least. Though it's not a traditional Thanksgiving dessert, this rustic tart is really a perfect addition. The baked apple slices are tender and caramelized at the edges, the almonds are crunchy and sweet, and the crust is thin and beautifully browned.

TO MAKE THE TART DOUGH

Combine the flour, salt, and sugar in a food processor fitted with the metal blade. Add the butter and shortening, and pulse until the mixture resembles coarse meal. Add the sour cream and water, and process for a few seconds, just until a ball of dough begins to form. Do not overprocess. (To make the dough by hand, place the dry ingredients in a large bowl, and use a pastry blender to cut the butter and shortening into the flour mixture. Add the sour cream and ice water, and mix just until it comes together and forms a mass.)

Transfer the dough to a floured work surface, gathering all the loose bits, and form into a disk about 1 inch thick. Wrap in plastic wrap and refrigerate while you are making the filling. Position a rack in the center of the oven. Preheat the oven to 400°F. Have a large, unrimmed baking sheet ready, preferably nonstick.

> > >

MAKES ONE 12-INCH TART;
SERVES 8~10

TART DOUGH

2½ cups all-purpose flour, plus extra for dusting

1   teaspoon salt

1   tablespoon sugar

½   cup (1 stick) ice-cold unsalted butter, cut into small pieces

½   cup ice-cold solid vegetable shortening

⅓   cup sour cream

2   tablespoons ice water

TO MAKE THE FILLING

Combine the almonds, apples, butter, sugar, vanilla, cinnamon, and nutmeg in a large mixing bowl. Mix thoroughly to dissolve the sugar and blend in the spices. Set aside.

TO ASSEMBLE THE TART

On a lightly floured work surface, roll out the dough into a circle about 14 inches in diameter. (It is fine for the edges to be uneven; it makes the tart look more rustic.) Dust the work surface and dough with a little more flour, as necessary, to keep the dough from sticking. Roll the dough around the rolling pin, lift it over the baking sheet, and unroll the dough over the pan. Adjust to center the dough; excess dough will hang over the edges of the baking sheet. Mound the filling in the center of the dough, leaving a 2-inch border. Fold the border of the dough over the apples (the center of the tart is open). Pleat the dough and pinch to seal any cracks at the edges. Brush the crust with the milk, and sprinkle generously with sugar.

Place the tart in the center of the oven. Bake until the crust is really well browned and the filling is bubbly, about 50 to 55 minutes. Transfer the baking sheet to a rack and cool. When ready to serve, slide the tart onto a large platter, and cut into wedges. Sweetened whipped cream or vanilla ice cream makes a wonderful accompaniment.

FILLING

½ cup sliced almonds, toasted (see Cook's Note, page 141)

6 Golden Delicious apples (about 2½ pounds total), peeled, cored, and cut into thin wedges

3 tablespoons unsalted butter, melted

¾ cup lightly packed brown sugar

2 teaspoons pure vanilla extract

1½ teaspoons ground cinnamon

¼ teaspoon freshly grated nutmeg

1 tablespoon milk

Sugar for sprinkling

BITTERSWEET
CHOCOLATE **PARFAIT** WITH
A CRANBERRY-CHERRY
COULIS

Chocolate parfaits for Thanksgiving? There always seem to be family members, especially young ones, who simply don't like pumpkin pie. This dessert is for them! I've never seen a child who, when handed a spoon and a parfait glass layered with rich chocolate and thick puréed fruit, can resist digging right in. In fact, I've never seen anyone turn down this dessert.

You'll need 8 parfait glasses or goblets that will hold about 6 ounces. You can use your mother's or grandmother's goblets, but there are lots of alternatives if these glasses aren't among your family treasures. Consider using small glass bowls, glass ramekins, juice glasses, martini glasses, or even brandy snifters—something that showcases the layers is all that's needed here.

TO MAKE THE CRANBERRY-CHERRY COULIS

In a 2½-quart saucepan, combine the cherries, cranberries, sugar, and lemon juice. Bring to a simmer over medium heat. Reduce the heat if the berries start to splatter, and cook until the cranberries pop, about 10 minutes. Set aside to cool for 20 minutes. Transfer to the work bowl of a food processor and purée. Chill while making the chocolate mousse.

SERVES 8

CRANBERRY-CHERRY COULIS

1 pound frozen sweet, dark cherries, thawed, including the juice

1 cup fresh cranberries or frozen cranberries, thawed if frozen

½ cup sugar

1 tablespoon fresh lemon juice

TO MAKE THE CHOCOLATE MOUSSE

Break or chop the chocolate into small pieces and put in the top of a double boiler over barely simmering, but not boiling, water. (A mixing bowl set in a saucepan half full of simmering water is a good substitute.) When the chocolate is soft, stir in the egg yolks and cook just until the mixture is thick, about 1 minute. Remove from the heat. Add the butter, salt, and vanilla. Mix well, transfer to a large mixing bowl, and set aside.

In a large bowl, using a hand-held or stand mixer, beat the egg whites at medium speed just until foamy. Increase the speed to high, and as big bubbles give way to little ones, start adding the sugar, 1 tablespoon at a time. Beat until the whites form firm, glossy peaks. Using a rubber spatula, beat one-fourth of the whites into the chocolate to lighten the mixture. Gently fold the remainder of the whites into the chocolate.

TO ASSEMBLE THE PARFAITS

Have ready eight 6-ounce parfait glasses or goblets. Spoon enough chocolate mousse into each glass to form a 1-inch layer. Refrigerate for 10 minutes. Spoon a ½-inch layer of the coulis on top. Add another 1-inch layer of mousse and refrigerate about 10 minutes. Add a final layer of coulis. Refrigerate the parfaits, covered, for at least 4 hours, but preferably overnight. (The parfaits can be made up to 2 days ahead.) Serve chilled.

BITTERSWEET CHOCOLATE MOUSSE

6 ounces bittersweet chocolate

6 large eggs, at room temperature, separated

3 tablespoons unsalted butter, at room temperature

Pinch of salt

1 teaspoon pure vanilla extract

Scant ½ cup sugar

PERSIMMON PUDDING

When my friends and fellow cookbook authors Mary Corpening Barber and Sara Corpening Whiteford were growing up in North Carolina, Thanksgiving at their house wasn't complete without persimmon pudding. I made the recipe they sent me and became totally hooked. So did the rest of my family: I caught my husband and children rewarming the pudding for breakfast the day after Thanksgiving!

In the South and Midwest, the American persimmon *(Diospyros virginiana)* is readily found in the market during the fall. Those who live on the East and West Coasts are more likely to find two varieties of the Japanese persimmon *(Diospyros kaki);* one type has a pointed base, and the other is smaller and more spherical. Any of these will work just fine as long as the fruit is exceedingly ripe—so soft to the touch that it would land with a splat if dropped on the ground.

Preheat the oven to 350°F. Butter a 9-by-13-inch baking pan. Cut the persimmons in half crosswise and use a spoon to scoop out the flesh, discarding the stem and skins. Use the back of a spoon to press the flesh into a soft pulp. Measure 2 cups (freeze the rest or reserve for another use). Combine the pulp, sugar, eggs, and vanilla in a medium bowl.

In a large mixing bowl, sift together the flour, baking soda, baking powder, salt, and cinnamon. Add the persimmon mixture, one third at a time, beating well after each addition. Stir in the buttermilk, cream, and melted butter. Pour into the prepared pan and bake until nicely browned and slightly puffed at the edges, about 45 minutes. Serve warm, or rewarm just before serving.

SERVES 12~16

2 cups persimmon pulp (about 1 quart persimmons)

2 cups sugar

2 large eggs, lightly beaten

1 teaspoon pure vanilla extract

1¾ cups all-purpose flour

1 teaspoon baking soda

1 teaspoon baking powder

1 teaspoon salt

1 teaspoon ground cinnamon

1½ cups buttermilk

½ cup heavy (whipping) cream

2 tablespoons unsalted butter, melted

COOK'S NOTE

Though the pudding is plenty rich as is, it's traditional to serve a dollop of whipped cream on the side.

LEFTOVER

FAVORITES

TURKEY **STOCK**

When it is time to clean up and put leftovers away after Thanksgiving dinner, my husband assigns himself the task of "dealing with the turkey." He carefully carves whatever meat is still left on the carcass and arranges it in a container. While doing this, he sips wine and picks at the carcass, nibbling on those delectable morsels of meat that cling to the bone, which is precisely why he likes this chore. He also offers to chop the carcass into large chunks and store them in a separate container, and this delights me. Come Friday morning, while I'm shuffling around in slippers and sweat clothes, drinking my coffee, I open the refrigerator and pull out the chopped carcass ready for the stockpot. While some may head for the mall to tackle their Christmas lists, honestly, I'm happier lounging with the newspaper, watching the stock simmer.

Put the chopped turkey carcass in an 8-quart stockpot, and add cold water to cover, leaving 2 inches of space at the top of the pot. Bring to a boil over medium-high heat; then reduce the heat so that the liquid simmers steadily. Using a large spoon or soup skimmer, skim off the brown foam that rises to the top. After 5 minutes or so, the foam will become white, and no more skimming will be necessary.

Add all the remaining ingredients. Partially cover the pot and adjust the heat so that the stock barely simmers. Cook the stock for at least 2 but preferably 4 hours, adding water, if necessary, to keep the bones covered.

MAKES **4~5** QUARTS

1	turkey carcass, chopped into large pieces
2	medium carrots (do not peel), cut into 2-inch chunks
1	large yellow onion (do not peel), cut in half
1	large rib celery, with leaves, cut into 2-inch chunks
1	teaspoon black peppercorns
1	bay leaf
6	sprigs fresh parsley

Using a slotted spoon, transfer the bones, meat, and vegetables to a large, fine-mesh strainer set over a large bowl to catch all the juices. Discard the solids. Pour the stock through the strainer into the large bowl. Let cool. (To cool the stock quickly, set the bowl in a larger one filled with ice water, or fill a sink with about 2 inches of ice water.) Stir the stock, occasionally, to help cool it down. Cover and refrigerate overnight.

The next day, lift and scrape the congealed fat from the surface using a large spoon. Discard the fat. Store the stock, covered, in the refrigerator for up to 3 days. To keep longer, transfer to a freezer container or several small containers, allowing 1 inch of headspace, and freeze for up to 6 months.

VARIATION: CHICKEN STOCK

Follow the recipe for Turkey Stock, substituting 3 quarts (about 3 pounds) chicken parts for the turkey carcass.

COOK'S NOTE

Making your own stock is a snap and there is just no comparison between homemade stock and canned chicken broth. Every time you buy a whole chicken or cut-up parts, save the neck, wing tips, back, rib (breast) bones, gizzards, heart, and tail—all the leftover parts except the liver— and store them in a 1-gallon lock-top storage bag in your freezer. (Date the bag and label it "for stock.") Keep adding to it, and when the bag is full, make a pot of homemade stock.

ROAST TURKEY
AND WINTER VEGETABLE
CHOWDER

SERVES 8

What better way to use up leftover turkey than in a hearty, chock-full-of-vegetables chowder. Walk the produce aisles and see what vegetables look fresh. Butternut squash is always firm and plentiful in winter. Choose Swiss chard, with either red or pale white ribs, or use kale. Red potatoes and onions are always stacked high. Though zucchini is overly abundant in summer, it's in the market year-round and is a great last-minute addition to the pot. When you serve this soup with a loaf of crusty French bread, you've got a perfect one-course meal.

In a heavy 6- to 8-quart saucepan, cook the bacon over medium heat, stirring frequently, until browned. Remove with a slotted spoon to a plate. Set aside. Pour off all but 2 tablespoons of the bacon fat, and return the pot to medium heat. Add the onion and celery. Sauté until the vegetables are soft, but not browned, about 3 to 5 minutes.

Add the potatoes, squash, and turkey stock. Bring to a boil, and reduce the heat to a simmer. Partially cover the pot, and cook until the potatoes are tender, about 15 minutes. Add the zucchini, Swiss chard, turkey, sage, thyme, and reserved bacon. Cook 5 minutes longer. Add salt and pepper to taste. Ladle the soup into warmed individual bowls or mugs, and serve.

3	slices bacon, diced
1	large yellow onion (10 to 12 ounces), cut into ½-inch dice
2	large ribs celery, cut into ½-inch dice
2	large red potatoes (about 8 ounces each), peeled and cut into ½-inch dice
1	butternut squash (about 1 pound), peeled, halved lengthwise, seeded, and cut into ½-inch dice
7	cups Turkey Stock (page 160) or canned low-sodium chicken broth
1	medium zucchini (5 ounces), cut into ½-inch dice
2	cups chopped deribbed Swiss chard leaves
2	cups ½-inch dice of roast turkey
1	tablespoon minced fresh sage
1	tablespoon fresh thyme
	Salt and freshly ground pepper

TURKEY POTPIE
WITH A BISCUIT CRUST

My grandmother used to make chicken potpies. Her turquoise, Formica-topped kitchen table would get a dusting of flour before she turned out the biscuit dough from the bowl. I'd keep my elbows on the edge of the table, hands at my cheeks, watching intently as she rolled out the dough. Sometimes she'd cut individual biscuits to top her potpies, and other times she'd make one big circle and lift it in one fell swoop onto the chicken filling. She baked her potpie in a 10-inch cast-iron skillet. As she grew old, though, her set of cast-iron pans got too heavy for her to lift. She gave them to me, and I use one to bake this dish. Any deep, oval or round baking pan will work—one just might hold more memories than another.

TO MAKE THE BISCUIT DOUGH
Combine the flour, baking soda, baking powder, salt, and pepper in a large bowl. Stir to mix well. Use a pastry cutter, two forks, or your fingertips to work the butter into the flour until the mixture resembles coarse meal. Stir in the buttermilk, and blend just until the dough holds together. Pat the dough into a ½-inch thick round, wrap in plastic wrap, and refrigerate while you are making the filling.

SERVES 6

BISCUIT DOUGH

2 cups all-purpose flour

1¼ teaspoons baking soda

1¼ teaspoons baking powder

½ teaspoon salt

¼ teaspoon freshly ground pepper

5 tablespoons ice-cold unsalted butter, cut into small cubes

¾ cup buttermilk

TO MAKE THE FILLING

Preheat the oven to 400°F. Have ready an 8-cup baking dish about 2 inches deep, or use a 10-inch cast-iron skillet with 2-inch sides.

In a 1-quart saucepan, bring the stock to a boil. Add the carrot and cook until crisp-tender, about 10 minutes. Using a slotted spoon, transfer the carrot to a plate and set aside. Turn off the heat under the stock.

In a 10-inch skillet, heat the butter with the oil over medium heat until the butter foams. Add the onion and sauté until it begins to soften, about 2 minutes. Add the mushrooms and sauté until they just begin to brown, about 3 minutes longer. Sprinkle the flour over the onion-mushroom mixture and stir to blend in. Slowly stir in the stock, bring to a simmer, and stir until smooth and thickened, about 2 minutes. Add the cream, stir to blend, and bring to a simmer. Add the reserved carrot, the turkey, and parsley, and stir to combine. Return the mixture to a simmer; then add salt and pepper to taste. Remove from the heat. Transfer the filling to a baking pan, unless you have cooked the filling in a cast-iron skillet.

Turn out the biscuit dough onto a floured work surface. Flour a rolling pin, and roll out the dough into a 10-inch circle. Carefully place the dough over the filling, centering it in the pan. Lightly press the edges of the dough against the sides of the pan. Brush the top of the dough with the milk. Cut 3 slits, each 2 inches long, in the center of the dough. Bake until the dough is nicely browned, about 25 minutes. Serve immediately.

FILLING

1½ cups Turkey Stock (page 160) or canned low-sodium chicken broth

1 medium carrot (4 ounces), peeled, and thinly sliced into rounds

3 tablespoons unsalted butter

2 tablespoons vegetable oil

1 small yellow onion (about 4 ounces), diced

8 ounces cremini mushrooms, wiped or brushed clean, stems trimmed, and quartered

2 tablespoons all-purpose flour

½ cup heavy (whipping) cream

3 cups ½-inch dice of roast turkey

½ cup minced fresh parsley

Salt and freshly ground pepper

2 tablespoons milk for brushing

TURKEY **TETRAZZINI**

SERVES 8

Tried and true, and a family favorite, I make this homey casserole every year. Sometimes, when it's not Thanksgiving, I'll roast a turkey breast just so I have leftovers to make tetrazzini. What comes straight from the oven to the table is a bubbly hot dish of al dente spaghetti with a scattering of tender poultry and bright green peas, covered with a silken cream sauce and topped with a crusty mixture of bread crumbs and Parmesan cheese. Forget the maligned version made in school cafeterias— this is the real thing.

Fill an 8- to 10-quart stockpot three-fourths full with water, cover, and bring to a boil. Add 2 teaspoons of the salt and the spaghetti, and cook until al dente (cooked through, but still slightly chewy), 8 to 10 minutes. Drain, rinse under cold water, and set aside.

Preheat the oven to 375°F. Butter a 9-by-13-inch baking pan. In a 10-inch sauté pan or skillet, melt the butter over medium heat. Add the flour and cook, stirring, until faintly colored, about 2 minutes. Gradually whisk in the stock until the sauce is smooth and thickened, 3 to 5 minutes. Whisk in the cream; then add the remaining 1/2 teaspoon salt, the rosemary, thyme, nutmeg, and pepper to taste. Stir in the turkey and peas, and heat through. Taste and adjust the seasonings; then remove from the heat.

Put the pasta in the prepared dish and spoon the turkey mixture over it. In a small bowl, combine the bread crumbs and Parmesan. Sprinkle evenly over the sauce. Bake, uncovered, until heated through and bubbly, about 20 minutes. Turn on the broiler and quickly brown the top of the casserole. Serve immediately.

2½	teaspoons salt
12	ounces spaghetti
6	tablespoons unsalted butter
6	tablespoons all-purpose flour
3½	cups Turkey Stock (page 160) or canned low-sodium chicken broth
¾	cup heavy (whipping) cream
2	teaspoons minced fresh rosemary
1	tablespoon fresh thyme
¼	teaspoon freshly grated nutmeg
	Freshly ground pepper
3½	cups ½-inch dice of roast turkey
10	ounces frozen green peas
½	cup dried bread crumbs
½	cup (2 ounces) grated Parmesan cheese

BLACK BEAN CHILI
WITH TURKEY

For chili lovers, here is a great way to use up leftover turkey.
Make this chili as hot or mild as you like by simply increasing
the amount of jalapeño or using mild green chiles instead.
Because chili freezes and reheats so well, this recipe makes a
large pot. A container of chili in the freezer is always a help for
busy weeknights. Make a batch of corn bread to serve alongside, or steam some rice and serve the chili on top.

Pick over the beans, removing any stones or other debris.
Rinse the beans and set them aside.

In a 4-quart or larger nonreactive heavy saucepan, heat the oil
over medium heat. Sauté the garlic, onions, green pepper, and
jalapeño chile until soft but not brown, about 5 minutes. Add the
chili con carne seasoning, brown sugar, coriander, cumin, thyme,
and oregano. Stir and cook 3 minutes longer. Add the beans, diced
tomatoes (including the juice), stock, and salt. Bring to a boil, and
reduce the heat to a simmer. Cover and cook for 1½ hours, or until
the beans are tender. Add the turkey and some pepper. Taste and
adjust the seasonings.

To thicken the chili, add 1 tablespoon of cornmeal at a time,
simmering for 3 minutes after each addition, until it reaches the
desired consistency. Garnish with cilantro and serve.

SERVES 8

1	pound dried black beans
3	tablespoons olive oil
4	large cloves garlic, minced
2	large yellow onions (about 12 ounces each), chopped
1	large green bell pepper, seeded, deribbed, and chopped
1	fresh jalapeño chile, seeded and finely chopped
¼	cup chili con carne seasoning or chili powder
2	tablespoons brown sugar
1	teaspoon ground coriander
2	teaspoons ground cumin
1	teaspoon dried thyme
1	teaspoon dried oregano
1	can (28 ounces) diced tomatoes in juice
5	cups Turkey Stock (page 160) or canned low-sodium chicken broth
1	teaspoon salt, or to taste
2	cups ½-inch dice of roast turkey
	Freshly ground pepper
	Cornmeal for thickening (optional)
4	tablespoons chopped fresh cilantro

CHILDREN'S TABLECLOTH

This no-sew project keeps the young ones busy and creates a family treasure at the same time. While family and friends are mingling and last-minute preparations for Thanksgiving dinner are in progress, have an adult trace the handprints of each child on the tablecloth. The spread hands look like the outline of a turkey, which the children can color and decorate with permanent fabric markers. Have them sign their names and you've got a keepsake for years to come.

Fold the fabric on the diagonal to form the largest triangle possible. Trim to form an exact triangle; when opened up, the result will be a 60-inch square. Heat an iron using the Cotton setting. With the wrong side of the fabric facing you, fold up the fabric along one side $1/2$ inch from the edge. Use straight pins, if needed, to secure the fold, and then press it. Repeat on the other 3 sides. On each side, fold the fabric over again, to create a hem $1/2$ inch wide. Miter the corners, trimming some of the folded fabric as needed. Slip the bonding under the hem, following the directions on the package. Iron the hem so that it bonds to the tablecloth.

Set the children's table with the cloth, and have a basket of permanent fabric markers ready. (Be prepared to supply each child with an old shirt or an apron to protect holiday clothing.) When guests arrive, have an adult trace the children's hands, using a ballpoint pen. Make sure the children spread their fingers wide to create a turkey image (the thumb will be the turkey's head). Let them color and decorate their turkeys, and then sign their artwork.

CHILDREN'S TABLE CENTERPIECE
An unfinished wooden toy wheelbarrow is available at craft stores. Fill it with fall leaves, tangerines, crab or lady apples, and grape clusters for a fun children's-table centerpiece.

CANDY CORN–FILLED VOTIVE HOLDER
Fill clean votive holders with candy corn for the children's table.

$1^{2}/_{3}$ yards unbleached chambray (60 inches wide; see Note)

Scissors

Iron

Straight pins

1 package fusible bonding web ($^{5}/_{8}$ inch wide)

8 to 10 autumn-colored permanent fabric markers (orange, burgundy, black, brown, yellow, red, green)

Ballpoint pen

NOTE
This tablecloth fits a standard card table (approximately 45 inches square). Adjust the amount of fabric you buy to fit your table.

TURKEY **ENCHILADAS**

This is a great way to use up turkey leftovers—especially a barbecued bird, because the smoky flavor of the meat pairs perfectly with Mexican ingredients.

Preheat the oven to 350°F. In a medium bowl, thoroughly combine the turkey, green onions, cream cheese, and 1 cup of the Jack cheese. Set aside.

In a blender or food processor, combine the salsa verde or tomatillos, chiles, cilantro, and cream. Blend until smooth.

Heat the oil in a heavy, 6-inch skillet over medium-high heat. Using tongs, carefully place 1 tortilla at a time in the hot oil, and leave it in for 5 to 10 seconds until softened. Turn the tortilla over and soften the other side. Drain over the skillet; then place on a plate lined with a paper towel. Place another paper towel on top and press to absorb the oil. Repeat until all 8 tortillas are softened and drained.

Place one-eighth (about ½ cup) of the turkey mixture in the center of each tortilla. Roll tightly and place, seam-side down, in a 7½-by-11-inch baking pan. Pour the salsa verde–cream sauce over the enchiladas, and sprinkle the remaining ⅓ cup of Jack cheese down the center. Bake until heated through and bubbly, about 20 minutes. Serve immediately.

SERVES 4

2 cups shredded roast turkey

2 green onions, white and green parts, thinly sliced

3 tablespoons cream cheese, at room temperature

1⅓ cups (5½ ounces) grated Monterey Jack cheese

2 cans (7 ounces each) salsa verde, or 1 can (13 ounces) tomatillos, drained (see Cook's Notes)

2 tablespoons canned chopped green chiles, drained (see Cook's Notes)

½ cup fresh cilantro leaves

⅔ cup heavy (whipping) cream

¼ cup vegetable oil

8 corn tortillas

COOK'S NOTES

After reading lists of ingredients on labels, and sampling many brands, I have become particularly fond of Herdez salsa verde. It is primarily crushed tomatillos with a bit of onion, chiles, and salt. If you can't find it, then use a large can of tomatillos.

I always have a can of chopped green chiles, sometimes labeled diced jalapeños, on my pantry shelf. They are easy to use in a baked sauce or egg dish. (For salsa, I prefer to use fresh chiles. Two tablespoons of chiles produce a moderately spicy sauce for this dish. If you like more fire on your palate, increase the amount by 1 or 2 tablespoons.)

ROAST TURKEY **SALAD**

WITH ANAHEIM CHILES
AND TOASTED PUMPKIN SEEDS

A day or two after a big Thanksgiving dinner, when there is plenty of turkey left over, a zesty and light main-course salad seems like a great idea. The flavors and foods of the American Southwest—chile, jicama, cilantro, and orange—combine deliciously with roast or grill-roasted turkey.

Preheat the oven to 350°F. Place the pumpkin or sunflower seeds in a single layer on a rimmed baking sheet and bake until lightly browned, about 15 minutes. Set aside to cool.

In a large mixing bowl, toss together the lettuce, chile, jicama, turkey, cilantro, and orange wedges. In a small bowl, combine the sour cream, mayonnaise, orange juice, salt, sugar, and pepper to taste.

Add the toasted seeds to the lettuce and turkey. Add the dressing, and toss the salad. Divide among dinner plates and serve immediately.

SERVES 5 AS A MAIN-COURSE SALAD

½   cup shelled unsalted pumpkin seeds or sunflower seeds

8   cups torn romaine lettuce leaves

1   large Anaheim chile (about 4 ounces), halved lengthwise, seeded, and cut crosswise into thin slices

8   ounces jicama, peeled and cut into 1 x ¼-inch matchsticks

3   cups 1 x ¼-inch matchsticks of roast turkey

½   cup chopped fresh cilantro

1   large navel orange, peeled, white pith removed, and cut into thin wedges

¼   cup sour cream

¼   cup mayonnaise

2   tablespoons freshly squeezed orange juice

½   teaspoon salt

½   teaspoon sugar

Freshly ground pepper

THANKSGIVING
MENUS
AND TIMETABLES

CHAPTER 8

SOME GENERAL THOUGHTS

PLEASE DON'T FEEL BOUND BY THE MENUS THAT FOLLOW.
THEY ARE MERELY POSSIBILITIES—COMBINATIONS THAT APPEAL,
TEXTURES AND FLAVORS THAT WORK WELL TOGETHER,
AND RECIPES THAT BALANCE THE COOK'S TIME.
CONSIDER THEM SPRINGBOARDS FOR YOUR OWN
GREAT AND INSPIRED MENUS.

MAKE LISTS

Make lots of lists. Your holiday entertaining will be easier for having done so. Make a grocery list and divide it according to the different stores you will have to shop at—butcher shop, bakery, wine shop, supermarket. Have a separate sheet of paper for the errands you will do each day. Keep a pen handy for crossing off the items you've purchased. I gain great satisfaction from an errand list completed and all checked off!

HAND OUT COOKING ASSIGNMENTS

Don't be shy: You don't have to be the only Thanksgiving cook. There is no doubt about it—cooking a Thanksgiving dinner is a lot of work. Just because the Pilgrims invited the Indians for the first harvest feast didn't mean the Indians came empty-handed—in fact, they hunted and cooked venison for the meal (and probably got to take home a few leftovers!).

CHECK EQUIPMENT AND DISHES

Figure out well ahead of time whether you have the right pots, sauté pans, baking pans, pie plates, and utensils required for the recipes. Do the same for dishes, silverware, serving pieces, and utensils, and even chairs! If you are short on plates, borrow some instead of trying to wash dishes between courses. Think about whether you are using a tablecloth or placemats. Are they clean? Do they need to be pressed?

ARRANGE YOUR FLOWERS OR TABLE DECORATIONS THE DAY BEFORE THANKSGIVING

Set your table as well. (It never fails—every time I feel harried when entertaining, it's because I didn't get the table set the night before.) You will have one less thing to think about.

ABOUT THANKSGIVING APPETIZERS

Keep these simple, or have guests bring them. You just need nibbles to stave off hunger—no one wants to fill up on cheese and crackers or heavy hors d'oeuvres. Stick to interesting olives—herbed French, niçoise, kalamata, and for the kids, black pitted ones. Have baby carrots, cherry tomatoes, interesting pickles, nuts, and marinated mushrooms. These are easy to arrange, they're light fare, and everyone likes them.

THINK ABOUT THE BEVERAGES YOU'LL BE SERVING

Wine suggestions are offered for each menu. Children always feel special and grown up when offered sparkling apple cider or apple juice served in wine glasses (use short-stemmed ones!). If you are planning to serve coffee and tea, measure the coffee ahead of time. Thermal serving carafes are very convenient.

WARM YOUR PLATES

Hot, delicious food deserves them. You can warm your plates in a clean dishwasher set on the dry cycle. Some dishwashers even have a plate-warming feature. Or, run the plates under very hot water, dry them, and wrap them in a terry towel until needed. Another option is to buy one of those plate-warming flannel bags (like an electric blanket for dishes).

THANKSGIVING DINNER
FOR TWENTY

Here's a traditional and elegant menu for a large crowd.
All of the food is perfect for a buffet. Order an 18-pound turkey.
You probably won't have a lot of leftover turkey, but there will
be plenty of food, given all the side dishes. If you want leftovers,
think about roasting an extra turkey breast, or two 12-pound
turkeys. Having two ovens would be really helpful for this menu.
Plan to make 2 batches of stuffing. Figure on 1½ batches of
the sweet potato gratin, and 2 batches of the mashed potatoes,
plus 2 batches of Carrot Pudding. The three different desserts
will give your guests tempting choices. An alternative is to make
2 pumpkin pies. A Côtes du Rhône, or a full-bodied Spanish red,
such as a Rioja or Ribera del Duero, would be delicious with
this meal.

NUTS, OLIVES, BABY CARROTS,
AND CHERRY TOMATOES

CLASSIC ROAST TURKEY
WITH JUNIPER BRINE

ITALIAN SAUSAGE, MUSHROOM,
AND SAGE STUFFING

MAPLE-GLAZED APPLE AND
SWEET POTATO GRATIN

CLASSIC MASHED POTATOES

CARROT PUDDING

GOLDEN CREAMED ONIONS

CHIFFONADE OF BRUSSELS SPROUTS
WITH DICED BACON AND HAZELNUTS

CRANBERRY CHUTNEY

MINIATURE MUFFINS WITH RICOTTA,
CURRANTS, AND DILL

SPICED PUMPKIN PIE WITH
PECAN PASTRY CRUST

CHOCOLATE GINGERBREAD WITH
SUGAR-GLAZED APPLES

PERSIMMON PUDDING

TIMETABLE

TWO WEEKS AHEAD
Order a fresh turkey (18 pounds).

ONE WEEK AHEAD
Make the Cranberry Chutney and refrigerate.

Make the Chocolate Gingerbread and freeze.

Make the Pecan Pastry Crust and freeze.

Buy and ripen the persimmons.

TWO DAYS AHEAD
Make bread cubes for the stuffing.

Cook and purée the carrots for the Carrot Pudding.

Cook and peel the pearl onions for the
Golden Creamed Onions.

ONE DAY AHEAD
Brine the turkey.

Put the pastry crust in the refrigerator to thaw.

Toast the hazelnuts for the Chiffonade of Brussels
Sprouts, with Diced Bacon and Hazelnuts.

Make the filling for the Spiced Pumpkin Pie and
refrigerate.

EIGHT HOURS AHEAD
Thaw the Chocolate Gingerbread.

Chop the vegetables for the turkey and stuffing.

Assemble and bake the Spiced Pumpkin Pie.

Assemble the Maple-Glazed Apple and Sweet
Potato Gratin.

Make the Miniature Muffins with Ricotta,
Currants, and Dill.

FIVE HOURS AHEAD
Make the Persimmon Pudding.

Assemble the Italian Sausage, Mushroom,
and Sage Stuffing.

Assemble the Carrot Pudding.

Make the Golden Creamed Onions.

Rinse and prepare the turkey.

THREE AND A HALF HOURS AHEAD
Roast the turkey.

TWO HOURS AHEAD
Make the Sugar-Glazed Apple Wedges for the
Chocolate Gingerbread.

Bake the Maple-Glazed Apple and Sweet Potato
Gratin.

Arrange the appetizers.

ONE HOUR AHEAD
Make the Classic Mashed Potatoes and keep warm.

Bake the Italian Sausage, Mushroom, and Sage
Stuffing.

Bake the Carrot Pudding.

SHORTLY BEFORE SERVING
Make the gravy.

Sauté the Chiffonade of Brussels Sprouts
with Diced Bacon and Hazelnuts.

Reheat the Golden Creamed Onions.

FOR A DOZEN

Thanksgiving for a dozen makes for a lively affair: One big table surrounded by guests feels festive, but the amount of food needed will be manageable. This menu works well for the cook who likes to get things done in advance. The Barbecued Turkey frees up an oven, so this menu is perfect for a one-oven household. An Oregon or Carneros (California) pinot noir would be a delightful wine to serve with this menu; a Washington state sauvignon blanc would be delicious, too.

NUTS, WATERMELON PICKLES, MARINATED MUSHROOMS, AND BABY CARROTS

DELICATA SQUASH SOUP WITH PARMESAN CROUTONS

BARBECUED TURKEY

CHEDDAR AND JALAPEÑO CORN BREAD STUFFING

PRALINE SWEET POTATO CASSEROLE

CRANBERRY SALSA WITH LIME

SAUTÉED GREEN BEANS WITH SHALLOT CRISPS

HERBED BUTTERMILK BISCUITS

HOLLYE'S PECAN PIE WITH SPIKED CHANTILLY CREAM

PUMPKIN CHEESECAKE WITH A GINGERSNAP CRUMB CRUST

TIMETABLE

TWO WEEKS AHEAD
Order a fresh turkey (14 to 16 pounds).

ONE WEEK AHEAD
Make the Pumpkin Cheesecake with
a Gingersnap Crumb Crust and freeze.

Make the pastry crust for the pecan pie and freeze.

TWO DAYS AHEAD
Make the bread cubes for the stuffing.

Make the Parmesan Croutons for the soup
and store at room temperature.

Make the Delicata Squash Soup and refrigerate.

ONE DAY AHEAD
Brine the turkey.

Make the corn bread and store at room temperature.

Hard-boil the eggs for the stuffing.

Thaw the cheesecake in the refrigerator.

Make the Cranberry Salsa with Lime and refrigerate.

EIGHT HOURS AHEAD
Make the filling for the Praline Sweet Potato Casserole.

Assemble the ingredients for the praline topping.

Make the Herbed Buttermilk Biscuits.

Assemble and bake Hollye's Pecan Pie.

FIVE HOURS AHEAD
Assemble the Cheddar and Jalapeño Corn Bread
Stuffing.

Make the shallot crisps and trim the green beans.

FOUR HOURS AHEAD
Soak the hickory chips for the grill.

Rinse and prepare the turkey.

THREE AND A HALF HOURS AHEAD
Prepare the grill.

THREE HOURS AHEAD
Barbecue the turkey.

Make the turkey stock for the gravy.

TWO HOURS AHEAD
Make the Spiked Chantilly Cream for the pie
and refrigerate.

Make the praline topping and spread it
over the casserole.

Remove the Cranberry Salsa with Lime
from the refrigerator.

Arrange the appetizers.

ONE HOUR AHEAD
Reheat the soup.

Bake the Cheddar and Jalapeño Corn Bread Stuffing.

Bake the Praline Sweet Potato Casserole.

SHORTLY BEFORE SERVING
Make the gravy.

Sauté the green beans.

Warm the biscuits.

THANKSGIVING DINNER
FOR FOUR

Quiet and intimate, a Thanksgiving dinner for four gives you
the opportunity to slow the pace and enjoy several courses.
Start with a soup course; carve the turkey breast at the table
and pass the side dishes; have the salad after the entrée; move
to the living room to enjoy dessert and coffee. A full-bodied
chardonnay would be perfect with this menu, a Beaujolais,
for red wine lovers, would be delicious, too.

HERBED GOAT CHEESE WITH CRUDITÉS,
OLIVES, AND SPICED NUTS

PORTOBELLA MUSHROOM BISQUE

ROAST TURKEY BREAST FOR A SMALL
GATHERING

BREAD STUFFING WITH APPLES, BACON,
AND CARAMELIZED ONIONS

CARAMELIZED SWEET POTATO WEDGES

CRANBERRY-ORANGE RELISH WITH MINT

SPINACH, PEAR, AND SHAVED
PARMESAN SALAD*

DOUBLE-CRUSTED CRANBERRY-
BLUEBERRY PIE

TIMETABLE

TWO WEEKS AHEAD
Order a fresh turkey breast (5 pounds).

ONE WEEK AHEAD
Make the pastry crust for the pie and freeze.

ONE DAY AHEAD
Make the Portobella Mushroom Bisque and refrigerate.

Make the bread cubes for the stuffing.

Place the pastry crust in the refrigerator to thaw.

Clean and dry the spinach for the salad and refrigerate.

EIGHT HOURS AHEAD
Assemble and bake the Double-Crusted Cranberry-Blueberry Pie.

Assemble the Caramelized Sweet Potato Wedges.

Make the Cranberry-Orange Relish with Mint (add the mint later).

FIVE HOURS AHEAD
Assemble the Bread Stuffing with Apples, Bacon, and Caramelized Onions.

THREE HOURS AHEAD
Prepare the turkey breast.

Prepare the ingredients for the Spinach, Pear, and Shaved Parmesan Salad.

TWO HOURS AHEAD
Roast the turkey breast.

Bake the Caramelized Sweet Potato Wedges.

Assemble the appetizers.

ONE HOUR AHEAD
Bake the Bread Stuffing with Apples, Bacon, and Caramelized Onions.

Add the mint to the Cranberry-Orange Relish.

Reheat the soup.

SHORTLY BEFORE SERVING
Make the gravy.

*   If you are serving the salad after the entrée, toss it just before serving.

A THANKSGIVING WITH
VEGETARIAN GUESTS

This menu assumes you are having ten for Thanksgiving dinner, and are having a mixed crowd—some vegetarians and some turkey eaters—requiring two entrées. If you use vegetable stock in place of chicken broth in the bread pudding recipe, your vegetarian guests will be able to eat everything on this menu except the turkey and gravy. They'll enjoy that! An Oregon or Carneros (California) pinot noir would be a delightful wine to serve with this menu; a Chianti would be another good choice.

BUTTER PICKLES, PICKLED ONIONS, CRUDITÉS, SALTED CASHEWS, AND OLIVES

HERB-ROASTED TURKEY
WITH GIBLET GRAVY

CHESTNUT, LEEK, AND
FRESH HERB BREAD PUDDING

LASAGNA WITH SUGAR PUMPKIN, RICOTTA, AND FRIED SAGE LEAVES

PRALINE SWEET POTATO CASSEROLE

GRATIN OF FENNEL AND TOMATO

CRANBERRY MOLDED SALAD WITH PINEAPPLE, CELERY, AND ORANGE

ROASTED BEET SALAD WITH WALNUTS AND GOAT CHEESE

PUMPKIN POUND CAKE WITH FRENCH VANILLA ICE CREAM

BOSC PEAR AND TOASTED HAZELNUT TART

TIMETABLE

TWO WEEKS AHEAD

Order a fresh turkey (12 to 14 pounds).

ONE WEEK AHEAD

Make the Pumpkin Pound Cake and freeze.

Make the pastry crust for the tart and freeze.

TWO DAYS AHEAD

Prepare the chestnuts, if you are buying fresh ones, for the bread pudding.

Make the bread cubes for the bread pudding.

ONE DAY AHEAD

Brine the turkey.

Make the Cranberry Molded Salad with Pineapple, Celery, and Orange and refrigerate.

Make the Lasagna with Sugar Pumpkin, Ricotta, and Fried Sage Leaves and refrigerate.

Put the pastry crust in the refrigerator to thaw.

Thaw the Pumpkin Pound Cake.

EIGHT HOURS AHEAD

Assemble and bake the Bosc Pear and Toasted Hazelnut Tart.

Make the filling for the Praline Sweet Potato Casserole.

Assemble the ingredients for the praline topping.

Roast the beets, toast the nuts, and make the dressing for the salad.

FIVE HOURS AHEAD

Make the Chestnut, Leek, and Fresh Herb Bread Pudding.

Make the Gratin of Fennel and Tomato.

Rinse and prepare the turkey.

THREE AND A HALF HOURS AHEAD

Roast the turkey.

Make the stock for the gravy.

TWO HOURS AHEAD

Make the praline topping and spread it over the casserole.

Remove the lasagna from the refrigerator.

Arrange the appetizers.

ONE HOUR AHEAD

Bake the Lasagna with Sugar Pumpkin, Ricotta, and Fried Sage Leaves.

Bake the Praline Sweet Potato Casserole.

Bake the Chestnut, Leek, and Fresh Herb Bread Pudding.

Assemble the Roasted Beet Salad with Walnuts and Goat Cheese, but reserve the goat cheese.

SHORTLY BEFORE SERVING

Bake the Gratin of Fennel and Tomato.

Make the gravy.

Crumble the goat cheese over the salad.

Unmold the Cranberry Molded Salad with Pineapple, Celery, and Orange.

THANKSGIVING ON THE RUN—

EVERYTHING MADE WHILE THE TURKEY ROASTS

Strap on your roller skates—you're going to have a fast and fun four hours of Thanksgiving cooking. You can do it! A few compromises are needed. Buy dinner rolls; you need some sort of bread to fill out this menu. It is quicker to make a wild rice stuffing than a bread stuffing, which is why I chose it for this menu. As for dessert, you really have two options: either make a dessert in advance and freeze it (the Pumpkin Pound Cake and the Chocolate Gingerbread both freeze well), or buy a pumpkin pie. If you have time, set the table the night before. Relax, and pour yourself a glass of wine—a full-bodied chardonnay or a fruity merlot would be perfect with this menu.

MIXED NUTS, KALAMATA AND NIÇOISE OLIVES, BABY CARROTS, AND MARINATED MUSHROOMS

BUTTER-RUBBED ROAST TURKEY WITH AN APPLE CIDER GLAZE*

WILD RICE STUFFING WITH PINE NUTS, DRIED APRICOTS, AND FRESH HERBS

PURÉE OF YUKON GOLD POTATOES

SUCCOTASH OF CORN, CHANTERELLES, ZUCCHINI, AND SWEET RED PEPPERS

CRANBERRY-ORANGE RELISH

STORE-BOUGHT DINNER ROLLS

STORE-BOUGHT PUMPKIN PIE, *OR* PUMPKIN POUND CAKE WITH FRENCH VANILLA ICE CREAM, *OR* CHOCOLATE GINGERBREAD WITH WHIPPED CREAM**

TIMETABLE

TWO WEEKS AHEAD
Order a fresh turkey (12 to 14 pounds).

Make the Pumpkin Pound Cake or the Chocolate Gingerbread and freeze (optional).

ONE DAY AHEAD
Brine the turkey (optional).

FOUR HOURS AHEAD
Prepare the turkey.

THREE AND A HALF HOURS AHEAD
Roast the turkey.

Assemble the Wild Rice Stuffing with Pine Nuts, Dried Apricots, and Fresh Herbs.

Make the Cranberry-Orange Relish.

Prepare the ingredients for the Succotash of Corn, Chanterelles, Zucchini, and Sweet Red Peppers.

TWO HOURS AHEAD
Arrange the appetizers.

ONE HOUR AHEAD
Make the Purée of Yukon Gold Potatoes and keep it warm.

SHORTLY BEFORE SERVING
Bake the Wild Rice Stuffing with Pine Nuts, Dried Apricots, and Fresh Herbs.

Sauté the Succotash of Corn, Chanterelles, Zucchini, and Sweet Red Peppers.

Make the gravy.

Warm the rolls.

*   If you can manage to brine the turkey the night before Thanksgiving, that would be great. Otherwise, baste the turkey frequently, and don't overcook it!

** Skip the sugar-glazed apple garnish for this dessert and serve the gingerbread with a dollop of whipped cream or a scoop of ice cream.

INDEX

TABLE OF EQUIVALENTS

The exact equivalents in the following tables have been rounded for convenience.

LIQUID/DRY MEASURES

U.S.	METRIC
¼ teaspoon	1.25 milliliters
½ teaspoon	2.5 milliliters
1 teaspoon	5 milliliters
1 tablespoon (3 teaspoons)	15 milliliters
1 fluid ounce (2 tablespoons)	30 milliliters
¼ cup	60 milliliters
⅓ cup	80 milliliters
½ cup	120 milliliters
1 cup	240 milliliters
1 pint (2 cups)	480 milliliters
1 quart (4 cups, 32 ounces)	960 milliliters
1 gallon (4 quarts)	3.84 liters
1 ounce (by weight)	28 grams
1 pound	454 grams
2.2 pounds	1 kilogram

LENGTH

U.S.	METRIC
⅛ inch	3 millimeters
¼ inch	6 millimeters
½ inch	12 millimeters
1 inch	2.5 centimeters

OVEN TEMPERATURE

FAHRENHEIT	CELSIUS	GAS
250	120	½
275	140	1
300	150	2
325	160	3
350	180	4
375	190	5
400	200	6
425	220	7
450	230	8
475	240	9
500	260	10